AILBOX® The Education Center®

grades **PreK–K**

Seasonal Science

Easy-to-Manage and Fun-to-Do Seasonal Science Activities

Fall	Winter	Spring
Fall Weather	Winter Weather	Rain
Rocks	Sun and Shadows	Sprouts
Exercise	The Heart	Soil
Water	Ice	Birds
Colors	Insulation	Bubbles

Plus Ten Other Science Topics!

Writers: Lucia Kemp Henry, Dr. Suzanne Moore

Managing Editor: Cindy K. Daoust

Editorial Team: Becky S. Andrews, Kimberley Bruck, Karen P. Shelton, Diane Badden, Thad H. McLaurin, Sharon Murphy, Karen A. Brudnak, Sarah Hamblet, Hope Rodgers, Dorothy C. McKinney

Production Team: Lisa K. Pitts, Pam Crane, Rebecca Saunders, Jennifer Tipton Cappoen, Chris Curry, Sarah Foreman, Theresa Lewis Goode, Clint Moore, Greg D. Rieves, Barry Slate, Donna K. Teal, Zane Williard, Tazmen Carlisle, Irene Harvley-Felder, Amy Kirtley-Hill, Kristy Parton, Cathy Edwards Simrell, Lynette Dickerson, Mark Rainey

Table of Contents

www.themailbox.com

©2006 The Mailbox®
All rights reserved.
ISBN10 #1-56234-665-2 • ISBN13 #978-156234-665-2

Manufactured in the United States
10 9 8 7 6 5 4 3 2

Fall

Fall Is in the Air

Cooler temperatures, warmer clothes, colorful leaves…it must be fall! Invite your little ones to study fall weather and the changes that signal this new season.

Looking for Fall

Even if the autumn changes in your area are subtle, your youngsters will find signs that say, "Fall is here!" Usher in the season by taking students for a walk outdoors to search for sights that signal the arrival of autumn. Before your excursion, make a copy of the recording card on page 8 for each child. Staple each card to an individual piece of cardboard. Then give each child a crayon and a recording card before you head outdoors. As you walk, encourage students to search their surroundings for signs of fall in the animals, clothing, trees, and weather around them. (If signs of fall are scarce in your area, enlarge the pictures from the card, color them, cut them apart, and place them along your walking trail for students to spot.) As each child sees an item pictured on her card, have her color the picture. At the end of your walk, return to your classroom for a discussion of this crisp and cool new season.

Let's Talk (and Sing) About Autumn

After your nature walk, lead a discussion about the fall sights your little ones saw. Display a large leaf shape cut from yellow bulletin board paper. Ask students to name the fall things they saw—both items that were on their recording cards and items that weren't. Write students' suggestions on the leaf shape to create a fall vocabulary list. Then teach little ones the tune below. As you repeat the verse, replace the underlined words with words and phrases from the list.

Later, invite youngsters to draw fall scenes, incorporating some of the things they listed on the leaf shape. Post the drawings and the leaf shape on a bulletin board.

(sung to the tune of "Down by the Bay")

Oh, fall is here. It's everywhere!
We see the changes here and there.
Oh, we can see [the green leaves change].
Can you feel it everywhere? Fall is in the air!
Yes, fall is here!

acorns
colorful leaves
jackets   sweaters
yellow grass
chilly air
squirrels

Autumn Leaf Exploration

Little ones will jump at the chance to visit this discovery center! Set up a large kiddie pool on a painter's drop cloth inside your classroom. Half-fill the pool with fall leaves; then invite a small group of students to join you there. Encourage your young scientists to use their observation skills as they explore and talk about the leaves. Ask questions to stimulate students' thinking, such as the following: Where do you think these leaves came from? What do the leaves feel like? What colors do you see?

As the leaves become crushed, remove them. (They'll make wonderful mulch for a class garden!) Then put a new supply of leaves in the pool for further exploration.

Leaf Comparisons

Have youngsters take a look at leaves to sharpen their comparison skills. In advance, find two leaves of the same size from a maple, an oak, or another deciduous tree. Choose one that is mostly green and one that has changed to its fall color. (Or cut matching leaf shapes from green and red paper.) Ask students to tell you how the two leaves are alike (size and shape) and how they are different (color). If desired, repeat the process with other pairs of leaves. Later, place a pile of real or paper leaves in a center for little ones to sort and compare.

Did You Know?

In fall, the weather gets cooler and we have fewer hours of sunlight. The change in the amount of light tells deciduous trees that winter is approaching. Winter is a time of rest for these trees, and their leaves don't need the *chlorophyll* that helps them absorb sunlight and make food for the tree. The chlorophyll in leaves gives them their green color. So as the chlorophyll disappears, so does the green color, revealing the bright colors we associate with fall.

Here Are the Leaves

Teach your little leaf lovers this fall fingerplay to reinforce the seasonal changes in deciduous trees.

Here are the leaves up on the tree,	Hold hands up, palms out.
Just as green as they can be.	Nod head.
Here comes fall. The air gets cold.	Wrap arms around body; shiver.
The green leaves change to red and gold.	Hold hands up, palms out.
Here come the leaves, tumbling down...	Wave hands and arms.
No leaves on the tree.	Point up.
They're all on the ground!	Point down.

Frosty Observations

Have your youngsters spied frost on leaves, on the ground, or on car windows on a cold autumn morning? Try this experiment to demonstrate how fall's chilly temperatures cause frost to form. You'll need two identical clear drinking glasses and access to a freezer. To begin, set the two empty glasses on a table for students to observe. Point out that the glasses are identical and that both are empty. Leave one on the table and have youngsters watch as you place the other glass in the freezer. After 30 minutes or more, remove the glass from the freezer and set it next to the glass on the table. Encourage students to touch and compare the outside surfaces of both glasses; then have them speculate on why the glass from the freezer is covered with frost. Lead students to conclude that the cold temperature in the freezer caused the frost to form.

This Is Why

Frost forms when water vapor changes directly to a solid. The glass in the freezer becomes cold enough to cause the water vapor in the air around it to cool very quickly. This rapid cooling changes the water vapor touching the surface of the glass into tiny ice crystals.

Cool-Weather Clothing

Invite your young weather wizards to collect some data about fall temperatures—it's as simple as having them check out the clothes they're wearing! To prepare, copy, cut out, and personalize a set of the shirt patterns on page 8 for each child. To begin the activity, direct students wearing long-sleeved shirts to line up on one side of your classroom; have students wearing short-sleeved shirts line up on the other side. Explain that as the weather gets cooler, people tend to wear warmer clothing, including shirts with long sleeves instead of short ones. Ask your group to compare the number of students in each line to decide whether the weather outdoors is likely to be cool or warm. Next, give each child a shirt pattern to match what she is wearing (long or short sleeves). Have her color the shirt and then attach it to a two-column graph. Count the shirts in each column and discuss students' impressions about the weather based on their clothing choices. Make a new graph each morning to involve your whole group in the daily weather report. Isn't it cool when every child is dressed for scientific success?

Fall Weather Tune

Teach little ones this tune about the chill of autumn. If desired, have youngsters brainstorm synonyms for *chilly* to substitute in the first and fourth lines.

(sung to the tune of "Short'nin' Bread")

In the fall the weather gets [chilly, chilly].
In the fall the temperature starts to drop.
Get out your sweater! Get out your hat!
The weather's getting [chilly] now;
That's a fact!

Fall Changes

Wrap up your exploration of fall weather by inviting each child to put together a festive booklet about the changes that take place in autumn. For each child, duplicate the booklet cover, patterns, and pages on construction paper. (See pages 9–13.) Use an X-acto knife to cut out the circle on each student's copy of booklet page 4. Then read through the directions for completing the booklet and gather the necessary materials. Guide each child as he completes his booklet cover and pages; then help him sequence and staple his booklet together along the left side.

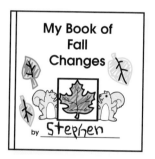

Cover: Cut out the cover. Color the leaf pattern, cut it out, and glue it to the page where indicated. Draw and color leaves around the title. Write your name.

Page 1: Cut out the page and the cloud pattern. Color the sky area on the page with a gray crayon. Glue the cloud to the page; then draw raindrops below the cloud with a blue glitter pen. Glue pieces of cotton ball to the cloud.

Page 2: Cut out the page. Color the tree trunk pattern, cut it out, and glue it to the page where indicated. Use a rubber stamp and an ink pad to decorate the tree with leaf shapes.

Page 3: Cut out the page. Color the moon pattern and cut it out. Color the sky area on the page with a gray crayon. Then glue the moon to the page. Draw a picture of yourself inside the house.

Page 4: Color the sweatshirt pattern; then cut it out. Glue the sweatshirt to the page where indicated. Draw leaves on the page. Tape a photocopy of your school photo to the back of the page so that your face shows through.

Recording Card
Use with "Looking for Fall" on page 4.

Fall Sights

seen by _____

Shirt Patterns
Use with "Cool-Weather Clothing" on page 6.

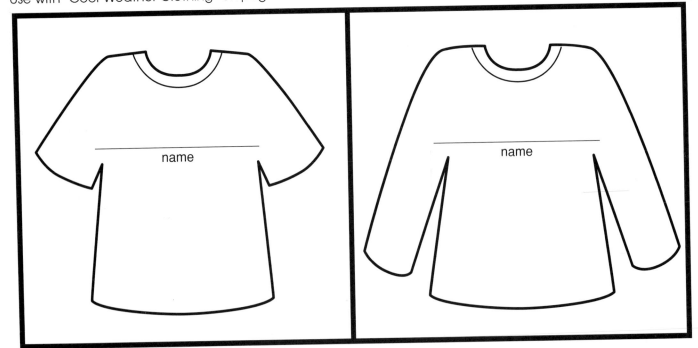

name

name

My Book of Fall Changes

Glue here.

by _____

 Color.

Cut.

Glue.

The weather changes. It gets colder.

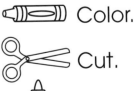 Color.

Cut.

 Glue.

2

Leaves change. Some leaves fall.

Glue here.

Whee!

Color.

Cut.

Glue.

Daylight changes. It gets dark early.

It's dark now!

3

 Color.

 Cut.

Glue.

My clothes change. I wear warm things.

Doh, warm!

Cut out.

Glue here.

4

Color.

Cut.

Glue.

Rocks Rule!

Bumpy, shiny, smooth, or tiny—rocks make for some interesting explorations! Treat youngsters to these rockin' activities and they're sure to agree: when it comes to science, rocks rule!

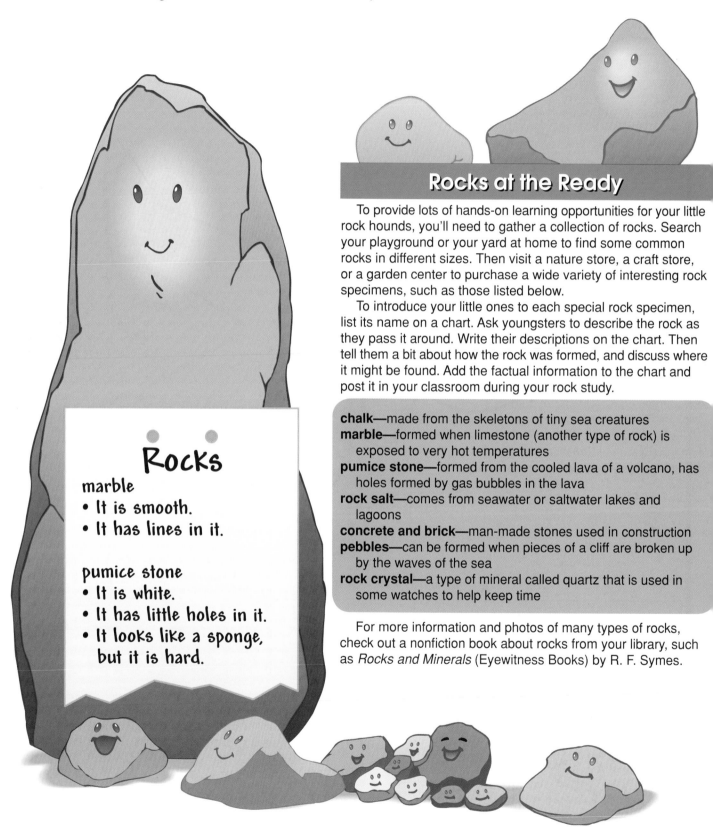

Rocks at the Ready

To provide lots of hands-on learning opportunities for your little rock hounds, you'll need to gather a collection of rocks. Search your playground or your yard at home to find some common rocks in different sizes. Then visit a nature store, a craft store, or a garden center to purchase a wide variety of interesting rock specimens, such as those listed below.

To introduce your little ones to each special rock specimen, list its name on a chart. Ask youngsters to describe the rock as they pass it around. Write their descriptions on the chart. Then tell them a bit about how the rock was formed, and discuss where it might be found. Add the factual information to the chart and post it in your classroom during your rock study.

chalk—made from the skeletons of tiny sea creatures
marble—formed when limestone (another type of rock) is exposed to very hot temperatures
pumice stone—formed from the cooled lava of a volcano, has holes formed by gas bubbles in the lava
rock salt—comes from seawater or saltwater lakes and lagoons
concrete and brick—man-made stones used in construction
pebbles—can be formed when pieces of a cliff are broken up by the waves of the sea
rock crystal—a type of mineral called quartz that is used in some watches to help keep time

For more information and photos of many types of rocks, check out a nonfiction book about rocks from your library, such as *Rocks and Minerals* (Eyewitness Books) by R. F. Symes.

Rocks

marble
- It is smooth.
- It has lines in it.

pumice stone
- It is white.
- It has little holes in it.
- It looks like a sponge, but it is hard.

Sing a Rock Song

Where do your rock hounds like to hunt for rocks? In the sandbox or deep in the dirt? In a favorite pond or along the road? Teach your youngsters this song to reinforce the idea that rocks are found in many places in our environment. Review your rock specimen chart to help students recall places where rocks can be found. To create new verses, use student suggestions for different locations to substitute in the third line of the song.

(sung to the tune of "Oh Where, Oh Where Has My Little Dog Gone?")

Oh where, oh where can we find some rocks?
Oh where, oh where can rocks be?
We can find some special rocks [in the sand]
If we just look and see!

Gee, We're Geologists!

One place your students are *sure* to find rocks is this rock exploration site at your sand table! Invite your students to play the part of geologists at this center set up for finding, identifying, and examining rocks. Provide children's hard hats, safety goggles, gloves, magnifying glasses, sand sieves, and clean paintbrushes at the center. Bury your rock specimens (gathered for "Rocks at the Ready" on page 14) in the sand. Photocopy pictures of the rocks from an encyclopedia or rock guide. Post the pictures near your sand table. Encourage your pint-sized geologists to unearth the rocks and then compare each one to the posted pictures to identify it.

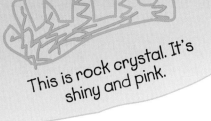

Deanne's Rock Report

This is rock crystal. It's shiny and pink.

Rock Reports

Since all good scientists document their findings, set up an area where your junior geologists can report on their rock explorations at your sand table. Provide students with rock-shaped paper, pencils, and crayons at a table near your sand area. After a student identifies some rock specimens from the sand table, have her take them to this documentation area. Ask her to draw a picture of each rock on a separate sheet of paper. Write her dictation as she describes each rock and how she identified it. Then staple the papers together behind an additional rock-shaped page to form a booklet. Title each child's booklet "[Child's name]'s Rock Report."

Rock Talk

If your little ones are eager to dig up more about rocks, read aloud *On My Beach There Are Many Pebbles* by Leo Lionni. This book will provide students with a close-up and creative look at rocks. During a second reading, ask students to identify the types of pebbles described by the author, such as strange, wonderful letterpebbles and peoplepebbles. List the words on a sheet of chart paper. Later, use the chart as a reference as students examine some of the rocks from your class collection. Hold up one rock and have a student give an adjective or descriptive name similar to those in the story. Review the words on your chart to help students with their descriptions. Repeat this process a few times. Then ask each child to choose a rock from your collection to hold. Have each child, in turn, give an adjective or descriptive name for his rock. Then ask each youngster to save his rock for use in the booklet activity that follows.

Here Is My Rock

Invite each of your students to create a descriptive booklet focusing on a favorite rock. To prepare, make a class supply of the booklet cover and text strips on page 19. For each child, cut four pages (sized to match the booklet cover) from white copy paper. Have each child cut out her booklet cover and text strips. Have her glue one text strip to the bottom of each of her four pages. Direct each child to complete her pages as described. Then help her sequence her pages behind the cover and staple the booklet together along the left side. Place each child's completed booklet in a zippered plastic bag along with her rock; then have her take the project home to share with her family.

Cover: Write your name on the line. Lay your rock on the cover and trace around it with a pencil. Then go over your pencil outline with a black marker.

Page 1: Lay your rock on the page and trace around it with a pencil. Next to the outline, draw a picture of an object that is the same size as your rock. Fill in the blanks in the text.

Page 2: Lay your rock on the page and trace around it with a pencil. Color in the outline with a crayon that matches the color of your rock. Fill in the blanks in the text.

Page 3: Lay your rock on the page and trace around it with a pencil. Put a small square of white tissue paper on top of your real rock. Gently color on the tissue with a crayon to create a rubbing. Glue the rubbing to the rock outline on the page. Fill in the blanks in the text.

Page 4: Lay your rock on the page and trace around it with a pencil. Use crayons and/or your pencil to make your rock outline resemble an object or animal. Fill in the blank in the text.

Opposite Rocks

Ask youngsters to further explore rocks' sizes, textures, and colors with this comparison activity. To prepare, sort through your classroom rock collection to find a few big rocks, small rocks, light-colored rocks, dark-colored rocks, rough rocks, and smooth rocks. To begin the activity, lay the rocks on a table and invite a small group of students to join you there. Ask a student volunteer to find a big rock and its opposite, a little rock. Ask another child to find a different pair of big and little rocks. Next, ask other students to find light- and dark-colored pairs and rough and smooth pairs. Continue until every child has had plenty of opportunities to compare a variety of rocks that have contrasting attributes.

Rock Attribute Song

Big and small, light and dark, rough and smooth…your rock lovers have found that rocks have lots of interesting attributes! Reinforce this descriptive vocabulary when you teach youngsters this song.

(sung to the tune of "The Mulberry Bush")

We know that rocks can be [big or small],
[Big or small], [big or small].
We know that rocks can be [big or small].
Rocks come in different [sizes].

(Repeat the verse two more times, substituting the attributes below for the underlined words.)
light or dark, colors
rough or smooth, textures

Rock-Sorting Center

Since rocks have so many attributes, they're perfect for sorting! To prepare a sorting center, fill a container with a variety of rocks and set out several large paper plates and some plastic magnifying glasses. Ask students at this center to sort the stones into groups by attributes: size, shape, color, texture, or any other attribute they choose! Have them place each group of rocks on a separate paper plate. Check in at this center periodically and ask students to describe the attributes they used to sort the rocks.

Which can has rocks?

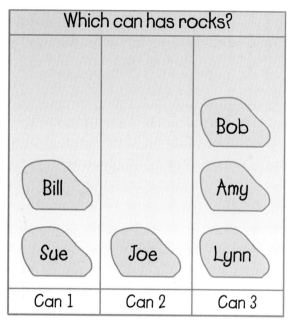

Can 1	Can 2	Can 3
Bill		Bob
Sue	Joe	Amy
		Lynn

There's a Whole Lotta Shakin' Goin' On!

Inquiring minds want to know—which can is full of rocks? That's the question in this fun inference activity. To prepare, cover three Pringles potato chip cans and lids with construction paper. Put some small rocks into one can, some pennies into another, and some popped popcorn into the third; then place the lids on all three cans. Label each can with a different number: 1, 2, or 3. Next, prepare a three-column graph as shown. Then cut a class supply of small rock shapes from gray construction paper.

To begin, show your group the three cans and explain that one of the three contains rocks. Explain that you're going to shake each can as they listen carefully. After you've shaken all three cans, give each child a rock cutout and ask her to write her name on it. Ask her to place her rock on the graph to represent her guess. Have a few student volunteers explain their reasoning. Then open all the cans and reveal the contents of each one. Did students' inquiry skills help them guess correctly? Repeat the activity on another day, if desired, substituting different materials for the pennies and popcorn.

Independent Inquiry Center

Invite your young scientists to create their own Inquiry Cans in this noisemaking, can-shaking center! To prepare, cover several snack-size Pringles potato chip cans and lids with construction paper. Also provide margarine tubs filled with pebbles, cotton balls, coins, dried pasta, dried beans, paper clips, and any other noisy (or not-so-noisy) items you have available. At this center, a child places pebbles in one potato chip can and fills the other cans with the materials of his choice. He then finds a friend to join him at the center. The partner shakes the cans and guesses which can holds the pebbles. It's true—two scientists have more fun than one!

Here Is My Rock

by _____

My rock is as _____ as a _____ .
(size)   (thing)

My rock is as _____ as a _____ .
(color)   (thing)

My rock is as _____ as a _____ .
(texture)   (thing)

My rock is shaped like a _____ !
(thing)

Fall Features

Fall into autumn with these colorful books full of seasonal sights.

When Autumn Comes

Written and Photo-Illustrated by Robert Maass

Does your part of the world enjoy a distinct seasonal change in autumn? Even if your youngsters encounter only subtle fall changes, this book will give the children a chance to study the bright leaves, sparkling frosts, and plump pumpkins of a northern autumn! After reading the book, have students recall fall weather, activities, plants, and clothing. Write student responses on a pumpkin-shaped chart. Substitute the words on the chart in the third line to create more verses for the song below. When you have sung several verses of the song, ask each child to name her favorite thing about autumn.

(sung to the tune of "Daisy")

Autumn is a wonderful time of year.
I like autumn. I'm glad that autumn's here!
Oh, [pumpkins] are right in season,
And that's a special reason
That autumn's neat. It can't be beat!
It's a wonderful time of year!

Autumn is a wonderful time of year.
I like autumn. I'm glad that autumn's here!
Oh, [raking] is right in season,
And that's a special reason
That autumn's neat. It can't be beat!
It's a wonderful time of year!

pumpkins
raking
scarecrow
jackets
trick-or-treat
corn
leaves
apple cider

Raccoons and Ripe Corn

Written and Illustrated by Jim Arnosky

The rowdy raccoons in this autumn tale enjoy a fall feast of tasty corn. Your little ones will harvest information with this Indian-corn observation activity. To complete the activity, gather the materials listed and have each child follow the steps below.

Materials needed for each child:
copy of page 22
ear of Indian corn (7" or less)
access to a supply of sticky dots
crayons
piece of yarn
glue
access to a balance scale and counting blocks
scissors

Steps:
1. Lay the ear of corn in the large box on the recording sheet. Use sticky dots, as shown, to record the length of the corn on the sheet.
2. Wrap a piece of yarn around the middle of the corn and then cut off the excess yarn. Glue the yarn on the recording sheet as shown.
3. Weigh the ear of corn on a balance scale. Count the number of blocks it takes to balance the scale; then draw the same number of blocks in the small box on page 22.
4. Remove a kernel from the ear of corn and then glue the kernel in the small circle.

Red Leaf, Yellow Leaf

Written and Illustrated by Lois Ehlert

Nothing symbolizes fall better than beautiful yellow, orange, and red autumn leaves. In this colorful picture book, Lois Ehlert's collage-style leaves seem ready to pop off the pages and blow away in the autumn breeze! As you read the book, give students plenty of time to study the pictures of the beautiful maple leaves.

Feel a Leaf

Use this inquiry activity to help your youngsters focus on the unique shapes of leaves. In advance, use the leaf patterns on page 23 to make tagboard tracers; then use the tracers to make a set of felt leaves. Arrange the felt leaves on a flannelboard; then place the tagboard leaves in your pocket. To begin the activity, secretly place one of the leaves from your pocket in a feely bag. Invite a child to put her hand inside the bag, feel the leaf, and then find the matching leaf on the flannelboard. Encourage the child to explain why she thinks the two leaves match; then have her take the leaf out of the bag to see if she is correct. Continue the inquiry process until each child has had a turn.

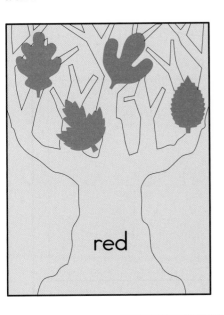

red

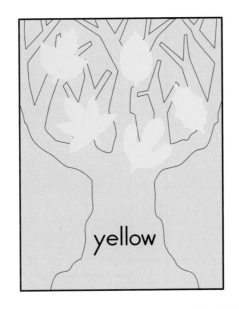

yellow

orange

Leaf Classification Center

Now it's time for your little leaf lookers to study the colors of fall foliage! In advance, make a red, a yellow, and an orange construction paper copy of the leaf patterns on page 23. Cut out the leaves; then place them in a basket. Next, make classification mats by making three copies of page 24 on tan construction paper. Label one mat "red," one mat "yellow," and one mat "orange." Place the mats and the basket of leaves at a center; then invite each child to use the mats to sort the leaves by color. To extend the classification opportunities, have each student sort the leaves by shape; then place the leaves on unprogrammed classification mats. Trees come alive with color!

Name _____

My Corn Report

My corn is this long.

My corn is this fat.

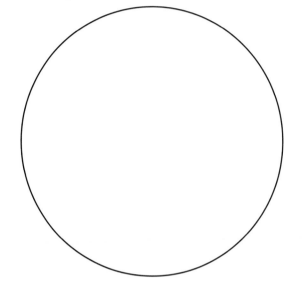

It weighs this much.

Here is a
corn
kernel.

Note to the teacher: Use with *Raccoons and Ripe Corn* on page 20.

Note to the teacher: Use with "Leaf Classification Center" on page 21.

Digging Into Dough

Fortify fine-motor skills and thinking skills as your students knead, roll, and press through these doughy science explorations.

Dough Delight

Dive into your dough study with a hands-on investigation that also reinforces language skills. In advance, follow the recipe below to prepare a batch of play dough. Then give each child a small ball of dough to roll, squeeze, and sculpt. As your students explore the dough, discuss with them how it feels, looks, and smells. Encourage students to describe different ways they handle the dough (roll, squish, pinch, etc.); then record their observations on chart paper. Save the chart and refer to it again in "D-O-U-G-H" below.

Delightful Dough
4 c. flour
½ c. iodized salt
1¾ c. warm water
few drops of food coloring

Combine the flour and salt in a bowl; then stir in the warm water and food coloring. Knead the dough for ten minutes. Keep the dough refrigerated in an airtight container.

roll

squish

pinch

D-O-U-G-H

Teach your students this song using the action words from the chart created in "Dough Delight" above.

(sung to the tune of "Bingo")

What are some things we do with dough?
What can we do with play dough?
We can [roll] the dough!
We can [roll] the dough!
We can [roll] the dough!
It's fun to [roll] the play dough!

Dry Discovery

Mix inferential thinking skills with exploration as your students dig into dough. To begin, invite a small group of students to observe as you mix together two cups of flour and one-half cup of iodized salt. Stir in teaspoons of warm water, one at a time, until the mixture begins to crumble. Then place a small amount of the mixture in a separate bowl for each child. Ask him to try to form a ball with his mixture. Then have him hypothesize why his mixture won't stick together. Lead him to conclude that the mixture needs more water. Next, provide the child with a small container of warm water and a teaspoon. Direct him to add water to his mixture, one teaspoon at a time, until the dough is sticky enough to form a ball. Allow each child some time to explore his dough; then have him place it in a personalized resealable plastic bag. Set the bags aside to use in "Air-Dried Dough" on page 27.

Detective Dough

Practice the scientific process skills of observing and inferring as your students investigate dough. Gather your students to observe as you mix two cups of flour, one-fourth cup of iodized salt, and 1¾ cups of warm water in a bowl. Stir the mixture and show students that it is too runny to form a ball. Lead students to conclude that adding more dry ingredients is necessary to make play dough. Gradually add two cups of flour and one-fourth cup of iodized salt to the mixture; then stir it to a doughy consistency. Refrigerate the dough in an airtight container to use in "Baked Dough" on page 27.

Just Dough It!

Teach your students this playful tune as you mix up a batch of play dough!

(sung to the tune of "Did You Ever See a Lassie?")

Have you ever made some play dough,
Some play dough, some play dough?
Have you ever made some play dough?
Let me tell you how!
You mix up some flour, some salt, and some water.
Have you ever made some play dough?
Let's make some right now!

Air-Dried Dough

Your students will begin thinking like scientists with this comparison activity. To begin, provide each child with the resealable plastic bag containing the dough from "Dry Discovery" (page 26). Have him divide the dough in half and then roll each half into a ball. Direct him to seal one ball inside his plastic bag. Then have the child place both balls on a personalized paper plate. Ask him to predict which dough ball will dry and harden first. Then place the plate on a table where it will be undisturbed. Encourage the child to check his experiment often to observe any changes. When the dough on the plate is hard and dry, have the child compare the texture and shape of the two balls. Then invite the child to hypothesize why the unbagged dough dried out.

This Is Why

The unbagged ball of dough was exposed to the air, which allowed the water in the dough to *evaporate*. The dough in the bag could not dry because the plastic blocked the water from evaporating into the air.

Baked Dough

Now that your students know that dough can be air-dried, try this experiment to show how heat can change dough. In advance, collect two snack-size resealable plastic bags for each child. Then make a class supply of page 28. Roll out the dough from "Detective Dough" (page 26) to a quarter-inch thickness. Then have each child use a cookie cutter to cut two circles. Ask the child to put one circle in a resealable bag and staple it to the left side of the recording sheet. Then help him complete the "Before" sentences. Next, have him use a toothpick to scratch his name into his second dough circle. Place all of the personalized circles on a cookie sheet and bake them at 300° until light brown. Remove the circles from the oven and let them cool. Then have each child put his baked dough into a resealable plastic bag. Staple the bag to the right side of the recording sheet, and then help him complete the "After" sentences. Discuss with your students the differences in size, texture, and color of the two samples. Lead them to conclude that the heat of the oven caused the dough to change.

Name __Tyler__

Baked Dough

Before the dough is baked it looks...
White, smooth, and flat.
It feels...
cool and soft.

Staple bag of unbaked dough here.

After the dough is baked it looks...
bumpy and brownish.
It feels...
hard.

Staple bag of baked dough here.

Tyler

Baked Dough

Before the dough is baked it looks…

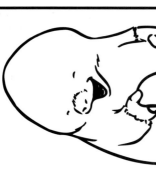

It feels…

Staple bag of unbaked dough here.

After the dough is baked it looks…

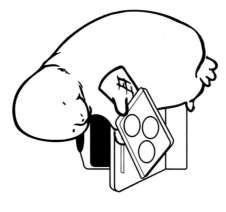

It feels…

Staple bag of baked dough here.

©The Mailbox® • *Seasonal Science* • TEC61005

Note to the teacher: Use with "Baked Dough" on page 27.

Energize With Exercise

Encourage your students to exercise the right to have strong, flexible, and fit bodies with these energizing activities!

Recess Exercise

One of the most important elements of a well-rounded fitness program is aerobic exercise. So set your youngsters on the path to fitness with a recess activity that promotes aerobics. After an outdoor recess period, have students discuss the things they did. Explain that some recess activities are *aerobic* exercises for the body. *Aerobic* means with air or oxygen. During aerobic exercise, the heart and lungs work harder to bring more oxygen to the body. Guide your youngsters to brainstorm recess activities that can be aerobic, such as running or jumping rope. Then write the activities on a graph. Over the next several days, encourage each child to engage in one of the activities during recess. After each recess period, invite each child to place a sticker on the graph to show which activity he chose. After a few days, tally the graph to determine which was the most popular activity.

Recess Exercise

jumping rope	running	tag

Did You Know?

The heart is a muscle! When we participate in aerobic exercise, we use whole muscle groups over an extended period of time. The heart beats more strongly in order to provide more blood to the other muscles at work. Aerobic exercise can strengthen many muscles, including the heart!

Follow the Leader to Fitness

Continue to promote aerobic endurance with this vigorous version of Follow the Leader. To begin, review the information in "Did You Know?" above. Then ask students to list aerobic activities or action words, such as *run, jump,* and *skip.* Record the words on chart paper and then point to each word as one child demonstrates the action. Next, have students form a circle and then appoint a leader to stand in the center. Ask the leader to choose one movement for each child to perform *in place.* Then have students follow the action of the leader for one minute. Allow students to rest for 30 seconds. Continue one-minute exercise intervals with different leaders. Add a little pep to each step with the following chant: "[Jumping, jumping], yes sirree! That's the exercise for me!" At the end of the activity, have students place their hands on their chests and try to feel their heartbeats. Are their little tickers thumping?

Flexible Fitness

In addition to aerobic activity, flexibility is another important component of fitness. Use this activity to stretch your little ones' muscles while stretching their minds! To begin, explain to students that our muscles are made of fibers that can be stretched, almost like elastic. Before stretching these fibers, it is important to slowly warm up the muscles. Lead your students in a warm-up activity, such as marching in place for a few minutes; then demonstrate a variety of stretching exercises. As your little ones stretch with you, encourage them to perform the movements slowly and avoid bouncing motions.

After stretching, help illustrate the importance of a warm-up with this activity. Show the group a chilled piece of caramel and try to stretch it. Next, roll the candy between both palms to warm it. Then try to stretch it again. Compare the ease of stretching the warmed candy to the muscles' ability to stretch after a warm-up activity.

This Is Why

Warm-up activities increase the blood flow to the muscles and make them easier to stretch. Regularly stretching our muscles helps keep them healthy.

Step Right Up!

Your students will march their way to stronger muscles with this small-group stepping exercise. In advance, visit a local health club and ask to borrow a few aerobic stepping blocks. To begin the activity, explain to students that another element of fitness is building strong muscles. Explain that climbing stairs helps strengthen the heart *and* builds strong lower-body muscles. Then have each child in a small group stand close to the front of a step. Instruct her to step up and stop, and then step down and stop. Ask her to practice slowly stepping up and down until she gets the feel for the movement. Then gradually pick up the pace. As students are stepping, have them try to identify which muscles are working. (Don't forget the heart muscle!) When students have mastered stepping, have them sound off the chant below as they exercise on the step.

If we work out every day,
We'll be strong in every way!
Step up.
One, two!
Step up.
Three, four!
Step up.
One, two,
Three, four!

Did You Know?
Stepping up makes leg muscles stronger because they lift the body up onto the step. Strong muscles are less prone to injury.

I Can Be Fit!

Have each child create his own guidelines for physical fitness with this booklet. To make one booklet, copy pages 32–34. Use an X-acto knife to cut along the dotted circles on each booklet page. Cut apart the booklet pages. Stack the pages in order; then staple them along the top. Tape a child's school picture behind the circle cutout on booklet page 5. Read through the directions below and gather the needed materials. Then help each child complete his booklet according to the directions.

Cover: Color the cover; then write your name on the space provided.

Page 1: Write a word for an aerobic activity (such as *run, jump,* or *skip*) on the line. Then draw yourself doing that activity.

Page 2: Write the word *stretch* in the space provided. Then draw yourself stretching.

Page 3: Write a word for a strength-building activity (climbing, biking) in the space provided. Then draw a picture of yourself doing that activity.

Page 4: Write your favorite fitness activity on the line. Then draw a picture of yourself doing that activity.

Page 5: Draw a picture of yourself. Then write three fitness activities that you like to do.

Fitness Finale

For a grand fitness finale, set up an exercise course that includes activities to build muscle flexibility, aerobic endurance, and muscle strength. To prepare, set up three playground or gymnasium workout stations (see suggestions below). Then have adult volunteers supervise each station. To begin, lead your youngsters in a warm-up activity and a stretching session. Then divide your class into three groups and assign each one to a different station. Have each group perform the activities at the station; then have the group try to guess whether the activities are aerobic, flexibility, or muscle-building activities. When each group has completed each station, have students walk a lap around the playground or gym to cool down.

runner's stretch

quadricep stretch

Aerobic Station
- jumping rope
- jogging in place
- jumping jacks

Strength Station
- push-ups
- lifting one-pound hand weights or unopened soup cans
- squats

Flexibility Station
- toe touch
- runner's stretch
- quadricep stretch

31

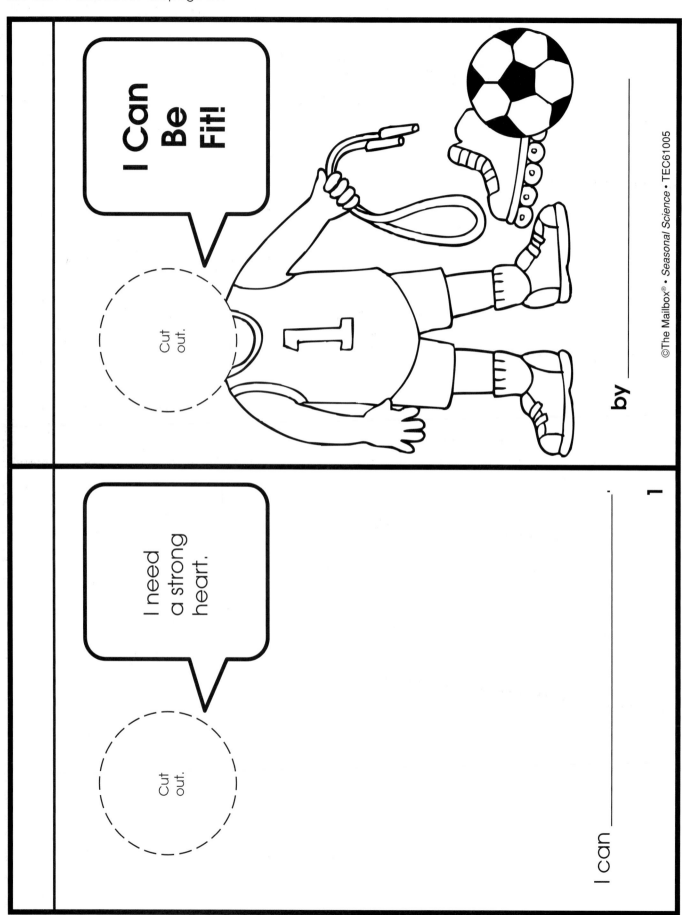

Cut out.

I Can
Be
Fit!

by _____

©The Mailbox® • Seasonal Science • TEC61005

I need
a strong
heart.

Cut out.

I can _____

1

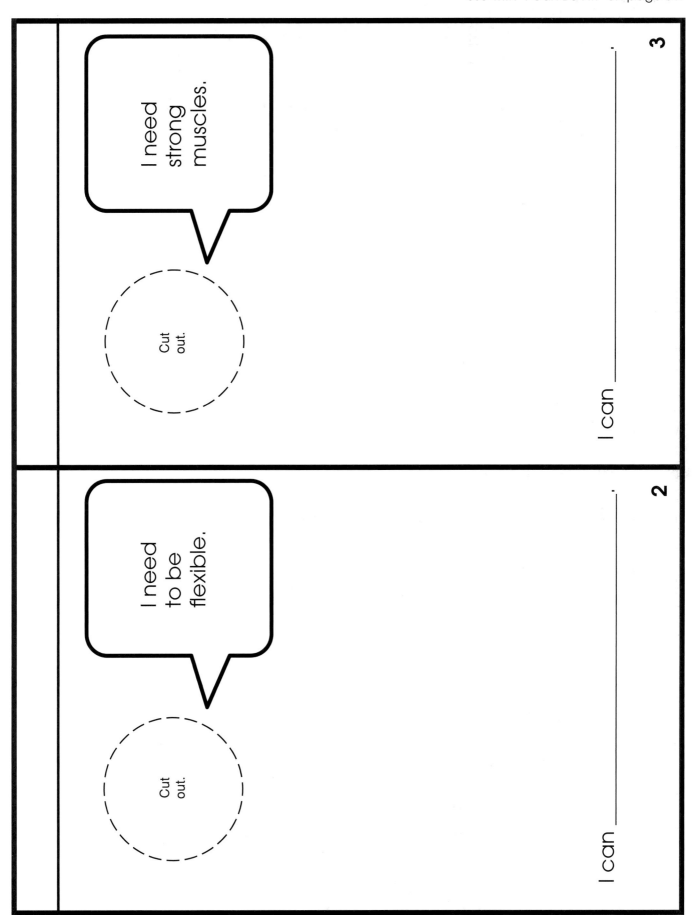

3

I need
strong
muscles.

Cut
out.

I can _____

2

I need
to be
flexible.

Cut
out.

I can _____

5

Here are three ways I can exercise.

Cut out.

4

This is my favorite fitness activity.

Cut out.

I can _____

Calling All Balls!

You can bounce it, throw it, catch it, kick it, and roll it. What is it? It's a ball!

Have a Ball!

Strengthen your youngsters' observation skills with this discovery activity! In advance, put a large ball in a black plastic trash bag and tie the bag shut. Have each student predict what might be in the bag. Next, have him feel the object through the bag and then make a guess. Reveal the bag's contents and initiate a discussion on the properties of the ball. Then arrange your students in a circle and pass around a variety of balls. Have students discuss ways that the balls are alike and different. Then call out a ball characteristic, such as rough, brown, or light. Instruct each student to roll his ball to another child when he hears a word that describes his ball. Continue playing until each child has had a turn to roll a ball.

Ball Characteristics

Your little ones will be moving and singing as they discover what balls can do! Sing the song to the right as your students pass a ball around the circle. After each verse, the child with the ball uses it to complete the action. Balls sure are "un-ball-ievable"!

(sung to the tune of "Pop! Goes the Weasel")

Balls can be heavy or light.
They can be smooth or rough.
So many colors they can be.
Roll the ball to me!

Balls are used for many things.
They can be kicked or tossed.
So many colors they can be.
Toss the ball to me!

Balls can spin and roll and bounce.
They can be big or small.
So many colors they can be.
Bounce the ball to me!

Behind the Bounce

Your little ones will bounce right into fun with this lively experiment! In advance, purchase two deflated beach balls at a discount store or an end-of-summer sale. Inflate one ball. Have each student take a turn bouncing the inflated ball. Then invite each child, in turn, to try bouncing the deflated ball. Encourage students to brainstorm reasons why only the inflated ball bounced. Your youngsters will be amazed to find out that air is behind all that bounce!

This Is Why

An inflated ball bounces well because it has enough air inside to push its walls outward. When the ball hits a hard surface, the side of the ball flattens against the air inside. If there is enough air inside the ball, it will push the side of the ball back out, making the ball bounce.

Up in the Air

Amaze your little ones with this ball experiment involving air! In advance, place a plastic funnel and a Ping-Pong ball at a center. Have each student put the ball inside the funnel as shown. Instruct her to blow downward onto the ball to see what happens. Then have her put her finger over the smaller opening and try blowing again. The ball moves! Invite your little scientists to brainstorm reasons why the ball moves.

This Is Why

When the small opening of the funnel is blocked, air flows around the ball and is trapped in the bottom of the funnel. The trapped air then pushes upward and moves the ball.

Round and Round It Goes

This interactive ball booklet will have your little ones practicing their positional word skills. To make one booklet, copy the booklet cover, pages, and patterns on pages 40–42. Have a child cut out each pattern, find the booklet page with the matching shape, and then glue the pattern onto the shape. Next, have the child personalize the cover and draw a self-portrait on booklet page 4. Direct the child to color and cut apart her booklet pages; then help her stack the pages in order and staple them along the left-hand side.

To make the movable ball for the booklet, cut a small circle from tagboard. Punch a hole in the top of the ball. Tie a ten-inch length of string through the hole; then tape one end of the string to the back of the booklet. Where will the ball go? Nobody knows!

Kyra's Ball

Round and round it goes. Where it will bounce, nobody knows!

Beside the dog, 1

in front of the tree, 2

under the bridge, 3

and over me! 4

From Here to There

Your students' scientific knowledge will be on a roll with this center activity. To prepare, place a supply of straws, a Ping-Pong ball, a large foam ball, and a golf ball at a table. Tell each student that he will be blowing air through a straw to try to move each ball across the table. Invite the child to predict which ball will be the hardest to move; then have him conduct his investigation. He may be surprised to find that the golf ball required the most air to get rolling. Lead him to conclude that the golf ball was the hardest to move because it was the heaviest of the three balls. Roll, ball, roll!

Ball Museum

Encourage your students to focus on the properties of different balls by setting up a classroom museum. Put a variety of balls on a table in your dramatic-play area. Invite your students to brainstorm ball categories—such as silliest, fuzziest, or biggest—and then have them create labels to match the categories. Have students vote for each category. Then display the winning balls next to their labels. Encourage students to make admission tickets, signs, and tour guide badges for the museum. Let the tours begin!

biggest

most
stitches

best
bounce

sillies

Rolling Along

Your youngsters will be amazed to find that different surfaces affect a rolling ball. Have each student experiment with an assortment of balls (Ping-Pong balls, small rubber balls, Wiffle balls, etc.). First, have him roll each type of ball on a grassy area. Then have him roll the balls on a sidewalk or a hard surface. Discuss each student's observations. Then have your group brainstorm why a ball rolls better on certain surfaces.

This Is Why

When a moving object touches another object, *friction* is created. A ball rolling over a grassy surface will move slowly because there is more friction. A ball rolling over a flat, smooth surface creates less friction, and therefore the ball rolls farther and faster.

Which Rolls Faster?

Involve your little ones in some further investigation of rolling balls. To prepare, gather a large and a small ball, such as a beach ball and a golf ball. Then make a ramp by taping a large piece of cardboard to the seat of a chair as shown. To begin the activity, provide each child with a copy of the recording sheet on page 43. Have students examine the balls and predict which one might reach the bottom of the ramp first. Invite two students to each hold a ball at the top of the ramp and then release the balls at the same time. Have each child record the results of the test by drawing a smiley face in the appropriate box on his recording sheet. Repeat the experiment, each time having students record the results on their sheets. Lead students to conclude that both balls rolled at the same speed. Amazing!

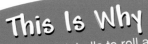

This Is Why

Gravity causes both balls to roll at the same rate. Their speed does not depend on their size or weight. Therefore, a large ball will reach the bottom of the ramp at the same time as a small ball.

Other Balls That Bounce

Introduce your little ones to balls that bounce for reasons other than air! In advance, gather several small solid rubber balls. Explain to your students that not all balls bounce because of air. Pass around the rubber balls and encourage each child to squeeze and bounce one of the balls. Invite each child to guess what is inside the ball that makes it bounce. Then explain that the ball is made of solid rubber. When the ball hits the ground, the outside of it flattens against the rubber inside. The rubber inside then pushes the side of the ball back out, making it bounce.

_____ 's
Ball

Round and round it goes. Where it will bounce, nobody knows!

©The Mailbox® • *Seasonal Science* • TEC61005

Beside the dog,

1

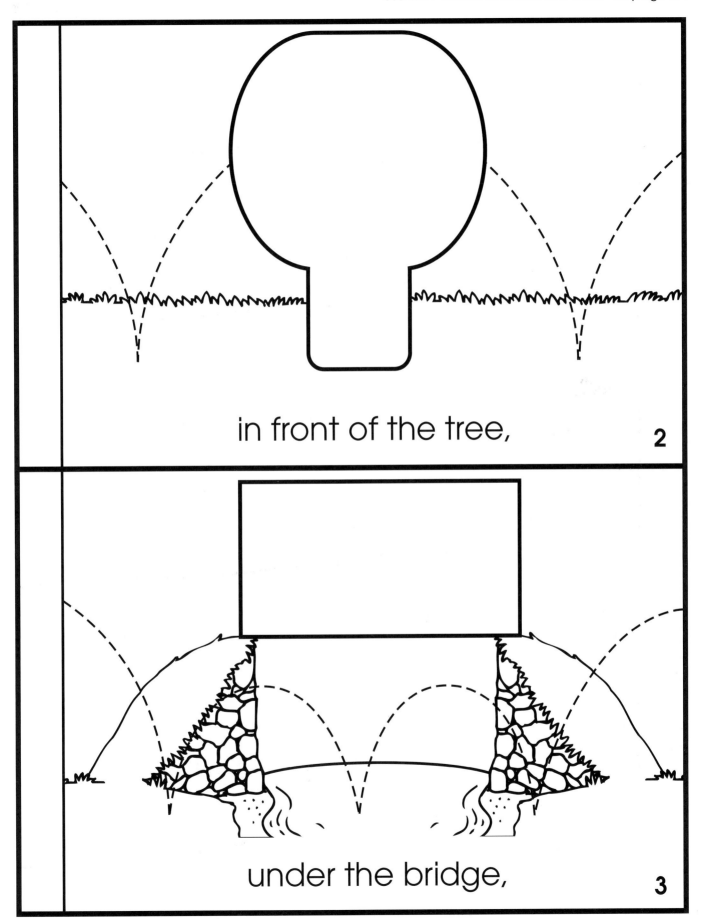

in front of the tree,

2

under the bridge,

3

Booklet Page 4 and Patterns

Use with "Round and Round It Goes" on page 37.

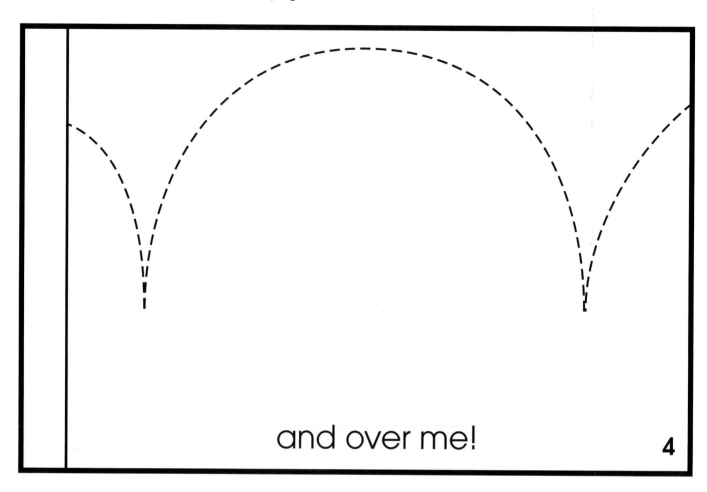

and over me!

4

Name_____

Which Ball Wins?

	🏀	◯	🏀◯ (tie)
1			
2			
3			
4			
5			

Note to the teacher: Use with "Which Rolls Faster?" on page 39.

Water Power

These water activities will whisk you and your students
away on a wild and wonderful learning experience!

It's Raining!

Get your youngsters moving in the right direction with this erosion
activity. In advance, put a thin layer of sand in your exploration table
(or in a large plastic tub). Make a rain sprinkler by punching several
holes in the bottom of a paper cup. Place the sprinkler at your exploration table, along with a small plastic pitcher filled with water. Invite
one student in a small group to form a mound of sand at the table.
Then have another child hold the sprinkler directly over the mound
as you pour water through the sprinkler. Encourage your students to
discuss their observations. Then explain that rain sometimes moves
loose sand or soil and that the process is called *erosion*.

This Is Why

When it rains over sand or soil, only
some of the water is absorbed. The excess
water flows downhill, carrying loose sand
or soil with it. This process is called erosion.

No More Erosion!

Your students will feel like scientific experts as they experiment with preventing erosion. In advance, cut several squares of
green tissue paper to represent grass and gather a small supply
of pebbles. To begin, have a small group of students predict what
might happen if rain falls on a mountain of sand covered with grass.
Then invite a student to build a mound of sand at the exploration
table. Have another child press the tissue paper squares on top of
the mound so that all parts of the squares are touching the sand.
Have a child use the rain sprinklers from "It's Raining!" (above) to
sprinkle water over the mound. Have students discuss their observations; then have them predict what might happen if rain fell on
a pebble-covered mountain of sand. Repeat the activity using
the pebbles. After this experiment, your youngsters will
understand that erosion *can* be prevented!

This Is Why

Plants, rocks, and trees help stop
erosion by holding the soil in place.

On the Move

Make way for water with this outdoor activity. To prepare, make a class supply of the reporting sheets on page 48. Gather the materials listed; then follow the steps below to perform this water energy experiment.

Materials needed:
6" x 8" piece of cardboard for each
  child (Cereal box panels work well.)
two 2-liter bottles filled with water
cookie sheet
bucket of soil
pencil for each child
wooden blocks
scissors
stapler

Steps:
1. Have each student cut her reporting sheets apart, stack them, and then staple them onto a cardboard back.
2. Take students outside with the needed materials.
3. Have student volunteers cover the back of the cookie sheet with a thin layer of soil.
4. Use a block to raise one end of the cookie sheet; then have a student slowly pour water down the cookie sheet in an even, steady stream.
5. Direct each student to make a sketch of the results on her first reporting sheet.
6. Repeat the experiment, using two blocks to raise one end of the cookie sheet.
7. Instruct each student to record the results on her second reporting sheet.

This Is Why

The higher one end of the cookie sheet is raised, the faster the water flows, giving it more energy. The more energy water has, the more soil it can move.

Sing a Song of Erosion

Reinforce the concept of erosion with this catchy song! In advance, duplicate the patterns on page 49. Color the patterns. Cut them out and then laminate them for durability. Place a piece of magnetic tape on the back of each pattern for use with a magnetic board. (Or use felt for a flannelboard.) As you sing the song below with your students, have a child point to each pattern when it is mentioned in the song. Drip, drop!

(sung to the tune of "Five Little Ducks")

Here's some soil lying on a hill.
Here's a rain cloud ready to spill.
When the rain hit the soil, then the soil did say,
"Rain on a hillside carries me away, me away, me away!
Rain on a hillside carries me away!"

45

Ensure a downpour of fun in your classroom with this booklet-making activity! To make one booklet, duplicate the booklet cover and text strips on page 50. Cut apart the text strips and glue each one to the bottom of a 5" x 7" sheet of construction paper. Read through the directions below and gather the necessary materials. Then have a child follow the directions to complete each booklet page. Help her stack the pages in order and then staple them behind the booklet cover.

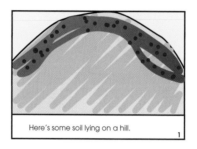

Cover: Write your name on the line. Color the picture.

Page 1: Draw and color a hill. Glue coffee grounds on the hill to represent soil.

Page 2: Draw a cloud on another sheet of paper. Color it gray; then cut it out. Glue it to the booklet page.

Page 3: Draw a cloud and raindrops above a hill. Glue coffee grounds on the hill.

Page 4: Draw and color a hill. Glue coffee grounds at the bottom of the hill to represent soil that was washed away.

Wonderful Waterwheels

Put a spin on learning with this waterwheel activity. To make one waterwheel, use a sharpened pencil to poke a hole through the center of a three-inch foam ball. Then insert a bamboo skewer through the hole. For safety, use masking tape to cover both ends of the skewer. Next, help a child insert four wooden craft spoons into the ball as shown. Sing the song below with your class as each child takes a turn holding her waterwheel under running water. Your youngsters will be amazed to discover that water can turn their waterwheels. Wow, that's power!

(sung to the tune of "The Wheels on the Bus")

My waterwheel goes round and round,
Round and round, round and round.
My waterwheel goes round and round
When water hits the spoons.

Moving Power

Your little hydrologists will have a blast moving an object with only water power! In advance, stock a center with a plastic tub of water, a turkey baster, and a lasagna pan with a Ping-Pong ball in it. Have a child visit the center and fill the baster with water. Then have him aim the tip of the baster at the ball and squeeze the bulb. Challenge him to refill the baster and move the ball using only water power. No hands allowed!

This Is Why

When the baster bulb is squeezed, the water inside is forced out. The force is enough to move the Ping-Pong ball. Other examples of water power include moving leaves with a hose and using the force of water to clean a sidewalk.

Reporting Sheets

Use with "On the Move" on page 45.

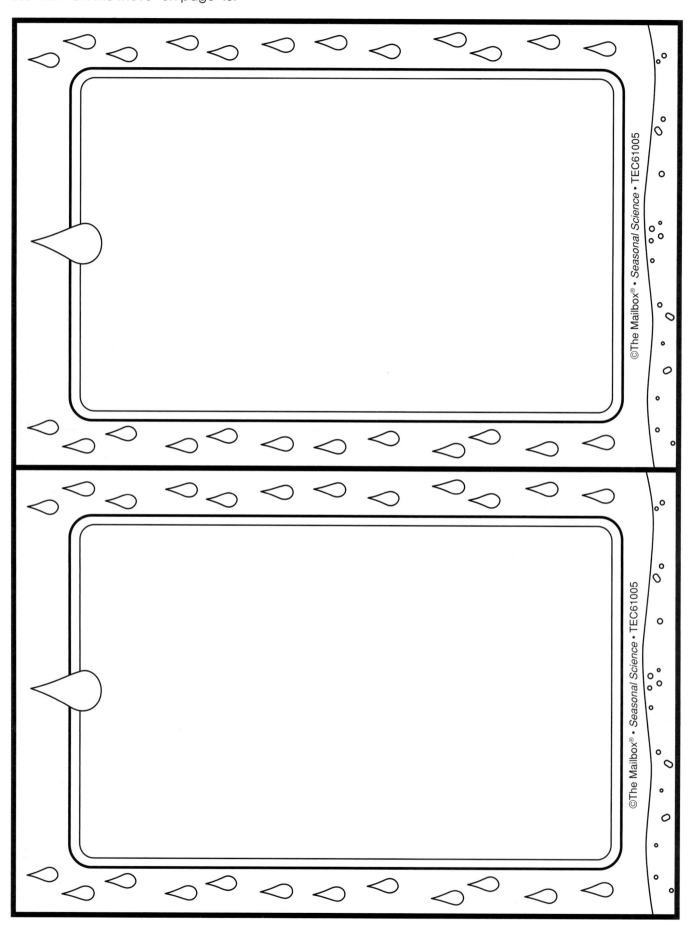

©The Mailbox® • *Seasonal Science* • TEC61005

©The Mailbox® • *Seasonal Science* • TEC61005

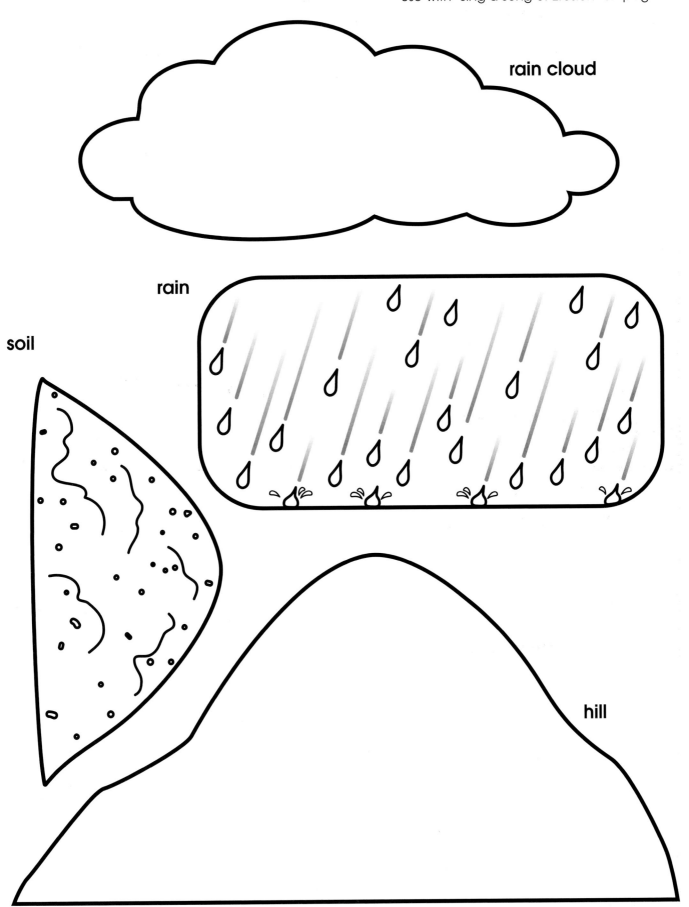

rain cloud

rain

soil

hill

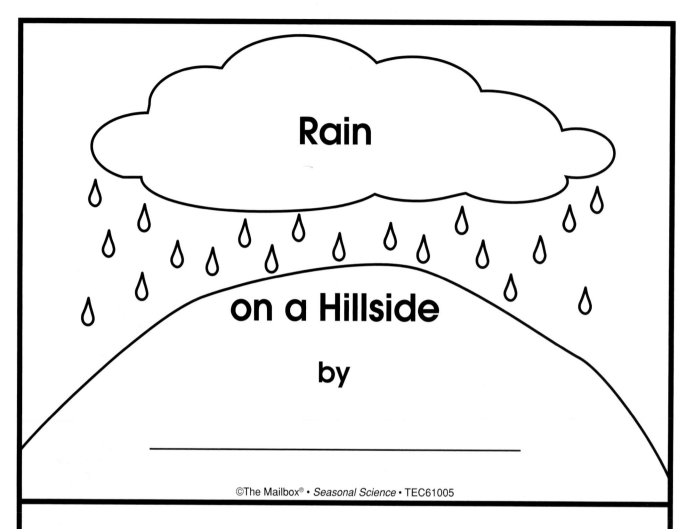

Rain

on a Hillside

by

_____

Here's some soil lying on a hill.

1

Here's a rain cloud ready to spill.

2

When the rain hit the soil, then the soil did say,

3

"Rain on a hillside carries me away!"

4

Color Quest

Fall is the perfect season to set your youngsters on a quest for color discoveries.

Lots of Colored Leaves

Kick off your color quest with a study of vivid autumn leaves. To prepare, gather a supply of red, orange, yellow, and green leaves. If leaves are not available, cut colorful leaf shapes from construction paper. During your circle time, have students sort the leaves by color. Next, divide students into four groups. Provide each group with a set of sorted leaves and a large sheet of paper that is the same color as the leaves. Direct the group to glue the leaves onto the paper; then write the appropriate color word on the paper. Display these leafy banners in your classroom throughout your color study.

yellow

orange

A Song of Colored Leaves

Reinforce color recognition with this song and movement activity. In advance, cut out and laminate construction paper leaves in a variety of fall colors. Next, have students stand in a circle, and provide each child with one leaf. Invite students to join you in singing the song below. When a color word is mentioned, encourage students with leaves of that color to move the leaves as if they are falling toward the ground.

(sung to the tune of "Clementine")

Lots of leaves in lots of colors,
Lots of colors all around.
Can you see the pretty [red] leaves?
See the [red] leaves falling down.

Repeat, substituting other appropriate color words for the underlined word.

Leaves of Green

Before they were red, yellow, orange and brown, most of those fall leaves were green! Set up this simple color-mixing center and have little ones create leaves as green as can be. To prepare, stock a center with yellow and blue food coloring, a few spray bottles filled with water, foil pie pans, and a supply of white coffee filters. Direct each child at the center to place a coffee filter in a pie pan. Then have him spray the filter with water until it is damp, but not soaked. Next, have the child squeeze three drops of yellow food coloring in the center of his filter. Then direct him to squeeze a drop of blue food coloring in the center of each yellow spot. To thoroughly mix the yellow and blue coloring, have the child spray his filter with a little more water. Encourage him to discuss any changes he observes. As an extension, invite the child to create different shades of green by experimenting with different amounts of yellow and blue food coloring. When the filters have dried, help the child cut leaf shapes from the filters. Then have him glue the leaves onto a piece of black construction paper.

Did You Know?

Green leaves get their color from a substance called *chlorophyll*. The chlorophyll helps leaves convert sunlight energy into a kind of sugar that provides food for the tree.

Did You Know?

Most leaves are *always* yellow and orange red! The green chlorophyll masks these other colors. In the fall, the leaves stop producing chlorophyll, and the yellow and orange red pigments are revealed.

Mixing Red and Yellow

When most leaves stop producing chlorophyll in the fall, they begin to change colors. Give your youngsters another color-changing experience with this activity. To begin, provide each child with a white construction paper leaf cutout. Help the child fold her leaf in half and then unfold it. Next, direct her to squirt several drops of yellow paint on one half and several drops of red paint on the other half. Have the child refold her leaf and gently rub the outside to mix the paint. Invite your little one to predict what will happen to the paint; then have her unfold the leaf. Encourage the child to carefully examine the paint; then lead her to conclude that wherever the red and yellow paint mixed together, orange paint formed.

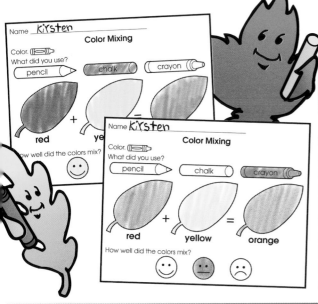

Pencils, Crayons, or Chalk?

Use this small-group investigation to find out which medium will blend colors the best: colored pencils, crayons, or chalk. To prepare, make three copies of the data sheet on page 56 for each child. Then provide each child in the group with the following: red and yellow crayons, red and yellow pieces of chalk, red and yellow colored pencils, and three data sheets. Have students recall the results from "Mixing Red and Yellow" on page 52. Invite each child to predict how well each medium will blend colors; then have her complete a data sheet for each medium. Compare the results of all three investigations and have your youngsters decide which artistic medium blended colors the best!

All Mixed Up!

Here's another interesting way for your crowd to investigate colorful mixtures. To prepare, fill two small clear plastic containers with water. Place several drops of red and yellow food coloring in one container and then stir the water until it turns orange. Next, place several red and yellow sequins in the second container and then stir the water. Your little ones may be surprised to find that the sequins do not change the color of the water.

This Is Why
The red and yellow food coloring mixed with the water and formed a new orange solution. The sequins did not combine with the water and form a new solution. Therefore, the color of the water did not change.

Purple Leaves?

Believe it or not, plants with purple leaves do exist! Several species of flowering plum trees have purple leaves that range in color from reddish purple to purple black. The *coleus* and the *dark opal basil* plants also have pretty purple foliage. If desired, find pictures of these purple plants in garden books and catalogs to show your youngsters. Then prepare for this positively purple activity!

To begin, provide each child with a sheet of fingerpaint paper. Then place a spoonful each of red and blue fingerpaint on the paper. Review the results from "Mixing Red and Yellow" on page 52; then lead students to conclude that mixing red and blue will create purple. Invite each of your little ones to use his fingers to mix the paint, and encourage him to discuss his observations. When the paint is dry, help the child cut leaf shapes from the paper.

Leaf Overlays

Have each child make this handy tool to help herself recall which combinations of primary colors (red, yellow, and blue) make which secondary colors (green, orange, and purple). To make one, you will need sheets of red, blue, and yellow acetate. (If colored acetate is not available, use clear acetate and red, blue, and yellow permanent markers.) Use the pattern on page 56 to make a tagboard leaf tracer. Then use the tracer to cut a leaf shape from each sheet of acetate. Provide a child with the acetate leaves, a small paper plate, and a paper fastener. Help the child punch a hole at the bottom of each leaf; then use the fastener to attach the leaves to the center of the plate. Direct the child to move one leaf over another to reveal a secondary color. For added reinforcement, have each little one use this leafy tool when singing the songs below.

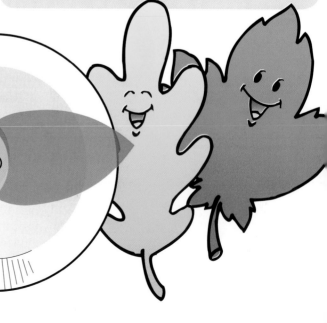

(sung to the tune of "Head and Shoulders")

Blue and yellow will make green,
Will make green!
Blue and yellow will make green,
Will make green!
The finest shade of green you've ever seen!
Blue and yellow will make green,
Will make green!

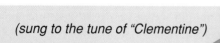

(sung to the tune of "Row, Row, Row Your Boat")

Red, red, red, and blue
Will make a purple hue.
Red and blue will mix to make
Purple through and through!

(sung to the tune of "Clementine")

Red and yellow
Will make orange
When you mix them all about!
Mix the red in with the yellow,
And some orange will come out!

Color Blending by the Book

Your little ones will love leafing through this booklet, which reinforces color-mixing concepts. To make one booklet, photocopy pages 57–59 on white paper. Next, use the leaf tracer from "Leaf Overlays" (page 54) to make two red tissue paper leaves, two yellow tissue paper leaves, and two light blue tissue paper leaves. Have a child follow the directions below to complete the booklet pages. When the pages are completed, help the child cut them apart, stack them in order, and then staple them along the left side.

Cover: Write your name on the line. Color the leaf.
Page 1: Use a crayon to color one leaf red, one leaf yellow, and one leaf blue.
Page 2: Brush water-thinned glue inside the leaf outlines. Place a blue tissue paper leaf on one outline. Place a red tissue paper leaf on the other outline. Brush a little more glue over the leaves until the colors in the middle begin to blend. Fill in the blank.
Page 3: Use red and yellow tissue paper leaves, and repeat the directions for page 2.
Page 4: Use blue and yellow tissue paper leaves, and repeat the directions for page 2.
Page 5: Use a crayon to color each leaf to match the color word below it.

A Leaf of Many Colors

Your color-smart students have explored the individual colors found in heaps of leaves. Now challenge each child to discover just how many colors he can find in a single leaf. In advance, duplicate the recording sheet on page 60 for each child. Then gather fall leaves that each contain different colors, such as green and yellow. If desired, laminate the leaves for durability. Place the leaves at a center along with the data sheets, a supply of crayons, and several plastic magnifying glasses. Invite each child to visit the center, choose a leaf, and then use a magnifying glass to examine it. Encourage the child to communicate her observations by completing a data sheet. What a vivid way to wrap up your color quest!

Leaf Pattern

Use with "Leaf Overlays" on page 54 and "Color Blending by the Book" on page 55.

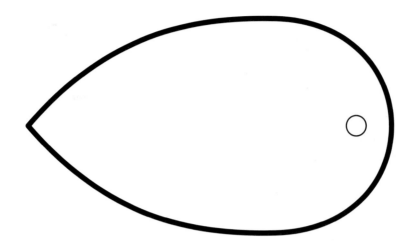

Name _____

Color Mixing

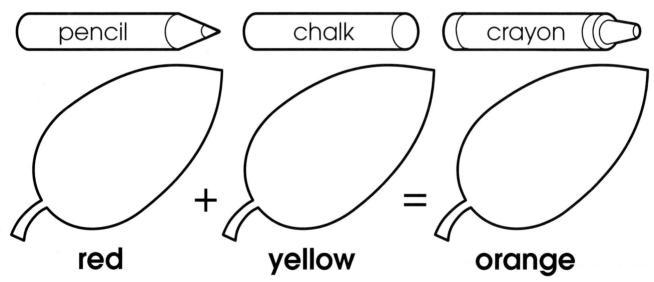

Color.

What did you use?

pencil   chalk   crayon

red   +   yellow   =   orange

How well did the colors mix?

©The Mailbox® • *Seasonal Science* • TEC61005

I Can Mix
Colors

by

_____

1

Red, yellow, and blue.

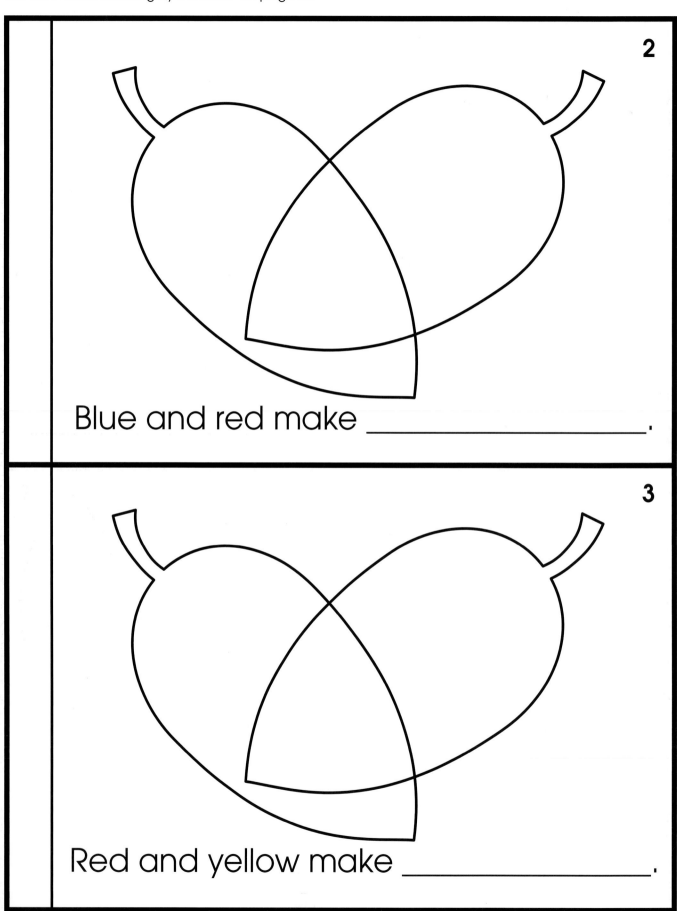

2

Blue and red make _____.

3

Red and yellow make _____.

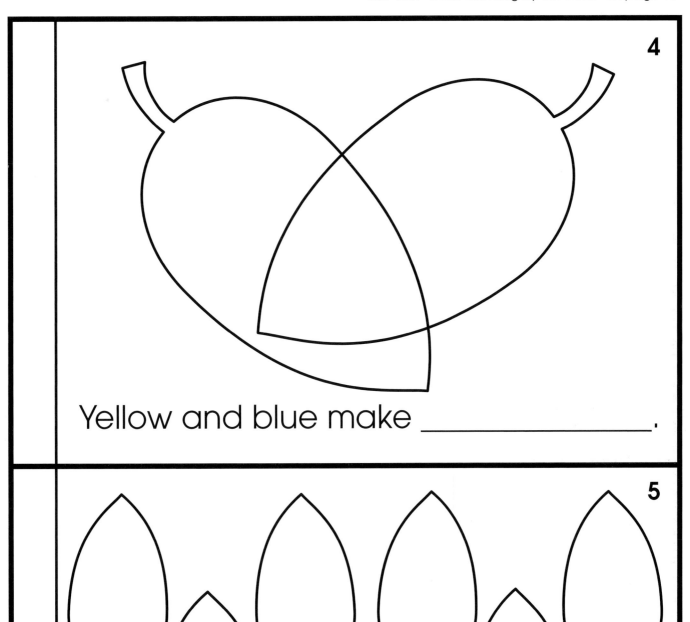

4

Yellow and blue make _____.

5

red   blue   purple   green

yellow   orange

The brightest colors I've seen!

Name _____

A Leaf of Many Colors

✏️ Trace your leaf.

Which colors do you see in your leaf?

🖍️ Color.

(green 🖍️) (yellow 🖍️) (red 🖍️) (orange 🖍️) (brown 🖍️)

🖍️ Color your leaf picture.

©The Mailbox® • *Seasonal Science* • TEC61005

60   **Note to the teacher:** Use with "A Leaf of Many Colors" on page 55.

Winter

Chill Out!

Is winter's chilly weather getting your youngsters down? Make the most of the cold by inviting each of your cool customers to investigate the seasonal weather that's all around!

Nippy Winter Weather

When winter arrives in most areas of our country, it puts a nip in the air. Introduce your youngsters to the wonders of winter weather with this simple sensory activity. On a chilly day, take your class outside and ask each youngster to describe what the cold weather feels like to her. To inspire student descriptions, prompt each child to describe how the cold feels on her face and hands. Next, return to the classroom and encourage each child to share one or two of the words that she used outside to describe the cold weather. Record student responses on a chart titled "What Does Winter Feel Like?" Later, reinforce this cold-weather vocabulary by teaching your chilly cherubs to sing the song below, using words from the chart to replace the underlined word in the third line.

(sung to the tune of "Are You Sleeping?")

I feel cold in, I feel cold in
Wintertime, wintertime.
Cold weather is [chilly], very very [chilly].
I feel cold; I feel cold!

Sensing Cold Temperatures

Turn the topic of cold into a more touchable activity! To prepare for a small-group investigation, place three bowls on a table. Secretly fill one of the bowls with very warm tap water, the second bowl with cool tap water, and the third with cold water that has been chilled in the refrigerator. Invite youngsters to observe the three bowls of water. Tell them that one bowl contains warm water, one contains cool water, and one contains cold water. Then challenge the group to discuss and identify the temperature of the water in each bowl *only* by looking. Next, encourage each child, in turn, to dip a finger into a bowlful of water and then describe the temperature of the water. Have him test each bowl in this manner. Your sensitive scientists will discover that "hands-on" measurement is a sure way to tell the difference between warm, cool, and cold!

Warm Winter Clothes

Keeping Out the Cold

When the going gets cold, the cold get going…to wrap up in warm winter clothes! Help students zero in on arctic-appropriate attire by asking them to name the types of clothes that they wear to go outside on a cold winter day. Next, look through a clothing catalog with students and have them identify the items that would be best to wear outside in winter. Also discuss with students why some clothes are suitable for cold weather and others are not. Follow up the discussion by having your little ones cut pictures of winter wear from more clothing catalogs. Then create a winter-wear collage by gluing the pictures to a large sheet of tagboard.

When It's Cold Outside

Teach your students this tune to bundle up the winter-wear vocabulary they've identified. Encourage youngsters to substitute the name of a different cold-weather clothing item each time they sing the song. "Snow" doubt about it—this song will be a hit!

(sung to the tune of "If You're Happy and You Know It")

When it's cold outside in winter, we wear [hats].
When it's cold outside in winter, we wear [hats].
In a nippy winter storm we wear clothes to keep us warm!
When it's cold outside in winter, we wear [hats].

I am outside on a cold winter day.

Symone

Winter-Day Wearables

Invite each of your cold-savvy students to communicate what she has discovered about warm clothing by having her draw a picture of herself in an outfit that's just right for a frosty foray outdoors! Give each child a large sheet of white construction paper and crayons; then ask her to draw and color a self-portrait to illustrate the caption "I am outside on a cold winter day." Display each child's completed artwork on a wintry-looking bulletin board along with the vocabulary chart generated in "Nippy Winter Weather" (page 62). Now that's winter wear with flair!

The Mittens I Wear in the Snow

Mittens are especially handy for playing outside on a cold, snowy day, so why not invite each child to don mittens for some imaginary indoor snow play at the sensory table? Fill the sensory table with white foam packing peanut "snow" and then have a small group of students put on colorful mittens and gather round! As your little ones play at the table, prompt them to discuss what color mittens would be the easiest to misplace in a pile of snow. To demonstrate, ask your youngsters to cover their eyes while you mix red, blue, green, and white felt mitten shapes in with the snow. Then challenge students to find all of the little lost mittens. Prompt youngsters to discuss the ease of finding colored mitten shapes compared with the ease or difficulty of finding white mitten shapes. Then ask them to imagine what color objects and animals would be hardest to see in the snow. Hmm—wonder where the white mittens are?

This Is Why

When an animal or object blends in with its background because it has the same color or pattern, it is very difficult to see. This phenomenon is called camouflage. Animals such as the snowshoe hare and the weasel rely on white winter fur to make it difficult for predators to spot them against a background of snow.

Lost in the Snow

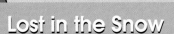

Reinforce the concept of camouflage by teaching your youngsters the words and movements of this action poem.

My little white mitten is lost in the snow.	*Show bare hand.*
I've looked for it high.	*Look up and point.*
I've looked for it low.	*Look down and point.*
Can't find my white mitten,	*Shake head no.*
And it makes me frown.	*Frown.*
For it's the same color	*Shake head yes.*
As the snow falling down!	*Wiggle fingers overhead.*
My little white kitten is lost in the snow.	*Cup hands; hold them out.*
I've looked for her high.	*Look up and point.*
I've looked for her low.	*Look down and point.*
Can't find my white kitten,	*Shake head no.*
And it makes me frown.	*Frown.*
For she's the same color	*Shake head yes.*
As the snow falling down!	*Wiggle fingers overhead.*

No Snow?

Don't get snow in your area? No problem—substitute very finely crushed ice in experiments calling for snow. Try crushing the ice in a blender to get a realistic snow texture.

White, Cold Snow

Here's a chilly investigation to help your little scientists sharpen their observation skills. To prepare, fill your water table with snow. Invite a small group of youngsters to look at the snow in the table. Then, as you list their observations on a snowflake-shaped chart, ask each child to describe what the snow looks like, its color, and whether it appears to be heavy or fluffy. Next, have your youngsters feel the snow. Again, list their comments as you ask them whether the snow feels dry or wet and whether it is warm or cold. Read the observations aloud; then post the chart near the sensory table. Hey—snow feels really cold and wet!

Snow

Snow is cold.

It's wet.

It's fluffy.

It makes me shiver.

Snow Melt

Chase

Chase

Take one cup of snow, add some observation skills, and mix in a dash of curiosity to make a cool science experience! Personalize a ten-ounce clear plastic cup for each student; then have him fill it with snow. Help each child mark the snow level on his cup by drawing a line on the outside with a red permanent marker. Have each child place his cup on a table. Set a timer so your students can inspect their cups every 15 minutes. Ask each child to describe what he observes as the snow in his cup melts. When the snow has melted, direct each child to mark the water level on the outside of his cup with a blue permanent marker. Prompt students to compare the levels of the red and blue lines; then have them discuss why the levels are different.

Guide children to understand that snowflakes are made of plain frozen water. Explain that snowflakes are surrounded by air, which takes up space. When the snow is scooped into the cup, air is scooped up too. The air is released when the snow melts. Therefore, the snow will always measure more *before* melting than it does afterward.

Pack It, Shape It, Build It!

Packed full of learning fun, this cool outdoor activity will have your little ones exploring the molding capabilities of snow. In advance, collect a variety of foam or plastic cups and containers to use for molds. Place your water table outside and fill it with snow. Arrange the containers around the table; then invite warmly dressed students to join you there. Show each child how to pack the snow into a container and then turn it over and jiggle it a bit to pop out the molded snow. Explain that when snow is pressed into the containers, air is pushed out and the snow crystals are forced close together. This is why the snow can be molded into different shapes. Encourage students to pack and mold more snow and then work together to construct a stunning snow structure!

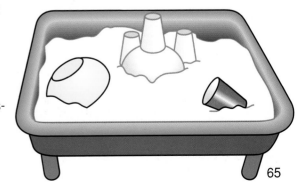

Charting Winter Weather

Since each child knows a bit about the attributes of winter weather, she'll be ready to take on the role of weather reporter! To prepare for one week of reporting the weather, make a class supply of the recording sheet on page 67. Staple a recording sheet inside a file folder for each child. On Monday morning, invite students to observe and discuss the weather using as many senses as possible—describing what the weather looks like, how it feels and sounds, and even what the air smells like! Have each child locate the Monday column on her page and then color in the appropriate box on her record. At the end of the day, discuss any changes in the weather that have occurred since the morning. Then challenge each child to predict what the weather will be like the next day. Have students repeat the process each day for the rest of the week. To reinforce what they've discovered about the field of weather forecasting, teach your youngsters to sing the song below.

(sung to the tune of "Did You Ever See a Lassie?")

Do you like to watch the weather,
The weather, the weather?
Do you like to watch the weather
When it's wintertime?

Oh, is the weather [snowy],
So wintry and [snowy]?
Do you like to watch the weather
When it's wintertime?

Repeat the song as desired, replacing the underlined word with a new weather word (such as *rainy*, *windy*, *foggy*, or *stormy*) each time.

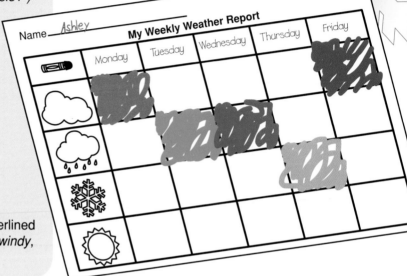

Winter Weather

Wrap up your study of wintertime with this wonderful little weather booklet. To prepare, make a light blue construction paper copy of pages 68–70 for each child. Have each child cut out her booklet cover and pages. Guide her to complete each page as described. Then help her sequence and staple her booklet along the left side. Conclude the activity by encouraging each child to share her booklet with a partner.

Cover: Write your name. Color blue raindrops. Stamp snowflake designs.
Page 1: Draw and color a picture of your face. Draw a warm hat on your head.
Page 2: Color the page dark blue. Make white snow dots with a cotton swab dipped in white paint.
Page 3: Color gray clouds. Glue on blue crinkle strips for rain.
Page 4: Draw and color a tree. Paint blue streaks to represent the wind.
Page 5: Draw and color a picture of yourself in winter clothes.

Name _____

My Weekly Weather Record

	Monday	Tuesday	Wednesday	Thursday	Friday
✏️					
☁️					
🌧️					
❄️					
☀️					

Note to the teacher: Use with "Charting Winter Weather" on page 66.

Watching Winter Weather

by _____

When I watch winter weather,
I look up at the sky.

1

I look for snow falling

2

or watch rain clouds roll by.

3

I look for wind blowing
a wintertime storm.

4

Then I go outside, dressed in
clothes that are warm.

5

Warm Up With Winter Foods

C-c-cold? Explore the cozy qualities of warm and hearty foods with these simple and savory ideas.

What Do You Eat?

Winter means cold weather and warm, filling foods. Discover what kinds of food your little ones enjoy eating during the winter by singing this tasteful tune!

(sung to the tune of "Six Little Ducks")

What do you eat when it's cold outside?
Which foods leave you satisfied?
Do you sip some soup or have some stew?
What warms you up when it's cold outside,
Cold outside, cold outside?
What do you eat when it's cold outside?

Blue Plate Special

After discussing favorite winter foods, invite each youngster to make a page for this yummy class book. Provide each child with a paper plate and a 12" x 18" sheet of colorful construction paper programmed with "I like to eat _____ when it's cold outside!" Ask her to draw her favorite wintertime foods on the plate. (Or have her cut pictures of those foods from magazines and glue them onto her plate.) Have her glue the plate to the center of her construction paper so that it appears to be on a placemat. Help her write to complete the sentence; then invite her to illustrate the placemat. Stack the completed pages between two covers and title the book "What Do You Eat When It's Cold Outside?" Bind the book along the left edge; then place it in your reading center for some really delicious reading!

I like to eat <u>oatmeal</u> when it's cold outside!

Did You Know?

Hot drinks and hot foods are good any time you feel chilled, especially in winter. They add heat to your body from the inside out. Dishes that contain corn, potatoes, and/or peas make you feel warmer…and keep you feeling warmer longer!

The Heat Is On

Stimulate your youngsters' observation and prediction skills with this nifty vegetable-cooking experiment. To begin, display clean, raw broccoli, carrots, and potatoes. Encourage youngsters to examine each of the vegetables and discuss its color and texture. Record student descriptions on a chart as shown. Next, invite students to brainstorm how boiling water might change each veggie's texture and color; then jot down those responses on the chart.

Keeping students a safe distance away, boil a pot of water. Chop each vegetable into chunks, add them to the pot, and cook for 30 minutes. Drain the vegetables and let them cool completely. Pour a portion of the cooked vegetables into a sensory table (or simply cover a student table with a plastic tablecloth). Working with one small group at a time, ask youngsters to observe the color of each vegetable as you record their responses. Next, invite your group to feel the cooked veggies, and record those responses also. Hey—it's okay to play with this food!

Vegetable	Raw	After Boiling (Cooked)
carrots	They're hard.—J'Quon They're orange and crunchy.—Dana	They're slippery!—Baxter They're not hard anymore.—Christina
broccoli	It's pretty and green like a tree.—Gabbie	It's darker and not pretty.—Gabbie You can bend it.—Chris
potatoes	They're white.—Sara They're not mushy.—Will	I can squish them!—Mary They're still white.—Dylan

This Is Why

When water boils, it moves around in the pot and transfers heat to the vegetables. This causes a physical change in the vegetables' texture due to heat breaking down some of the fiber, which gives vegetables stiffness. A chemical change occurs when broccoli is heated. The chlorophyll in the broccoli (the chemical in plants that makes them green) reacts to the natural acid in the water and turns the broccoli a drab, olive green color.

Soup's On!

Now that your youngsters know that heat can change vegetable texture, why not have them help make a tasty pot of tender, homemade vegetable soup? Using your favorite recipe, invite each student to bring a vegetable for the soup. On the designated day, have him predict what will happen to his vegetable's color and texture after it is cooked. Then chop each vegetable and have each child add his vegetable to the pot. Cook the soup as directed in your recipe; then invite your little ones to create the booklet in "Making Vegetable Soup" (page 73) while they wait. When the veggies are tender, serve each child a soup sample in a heat-resistant cup. Don't forget to ask him to check the texture and color of the vegetable he contributed. Did it change?

Making Vegetable Soup

Here's a booklet that will tempt youngsters' taste buds. Duplicate the booklet pages (pages 74–77) for each child; then cut the pages apart. Read the title of the booklet aloud and ask each student to write her name on the cover. Read the booklet aloud and then help each child complete her booklet according to the suggestions below. Have each child sequence her pages and staple them behind the cover. When each child has completed her booklet, encourage her to read it aloud to her classmates and then take it home to share with her friends and family members. Sounds like a recipe for reading to me!

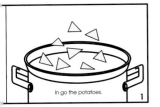

Page 1: Cut and glue manila paper triangles to represent potato chunks.

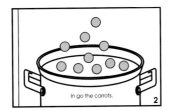

Page 2: Use orange sticky dots for carrot discs.

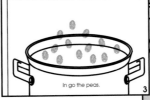

Page 3: Use a washable green ink pad to make green fingerprints to represent peas.

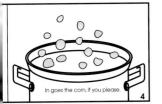

Page 4: Print corn kernels with a cotton swab dipped in yellow tempera paint.

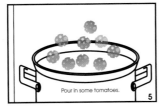

Page 5: Sponge-print red tempera tomatoes.

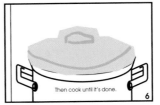

Page 6: Cut out a construction paper lid and glue it onto the pot.

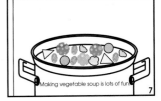

Page 7: Use a combination of the techniques given for pages 1–5 to make vegetable soup.

Chicken Soup Choices

Mmm, good! Nothing's better on a cold winter day than a bowl of chicken noodle soup. Discover which type of chicken noodle soup—canned or dehydrated—your little ones prefer with this tasty graphing activity. In advance, obtain several cans and pouches of chicken noodle soup, along with two small heat-resistant cups and a plastic spoon for each child. Also make a class supply of the soup bowl pattern on page 78. Label a bar graph as shown. To begin, encourage youngsters to describe the color and texture of the canned soup as you pour it into a pot. Next, pour the dehydrated soup into another pot and ask students how it looks different. Encourage your little soup lovers to compare the visual differences between the soups and predict which flavor will be liked best by the class. After preparing both soups, invite each child to taste them, keeping his preference a secret. Have him write his name on a copy of the soup bowl pattern. Invite student volunteers to glue the can label and the empty pouch to the graph. Then have each child reveal his preference by gluing his soup bowl in the appropriate column. Count the soup bowls in each column; then compare the results. Which is the preferred chicken noodle soup in your class?

MAKING VEGETABLE SOUP

by

_____

In go the potatoes.

1

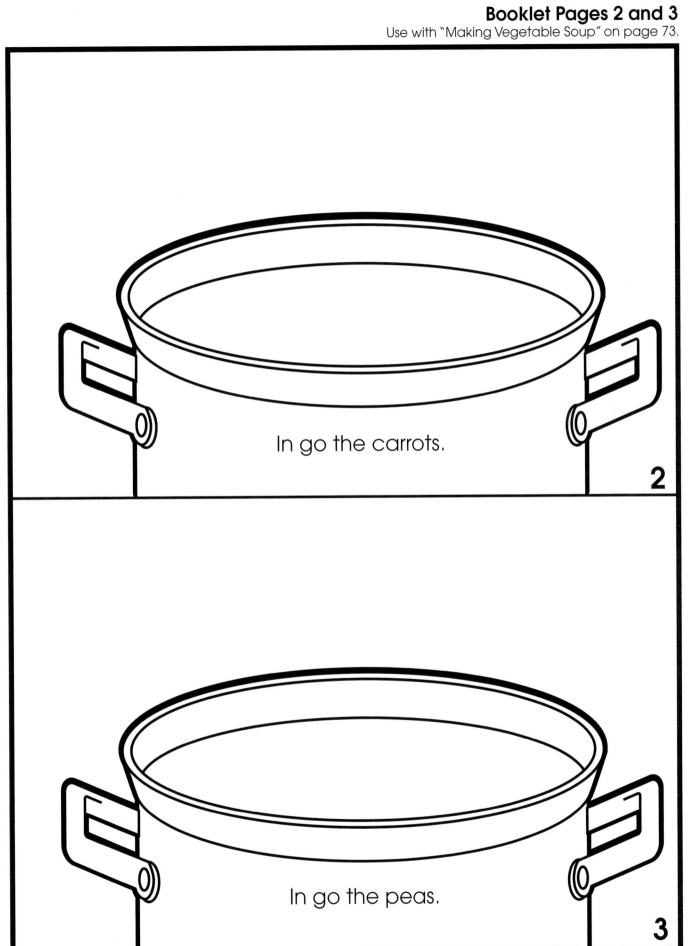

In go the carrots.

2

In go the peas.

3

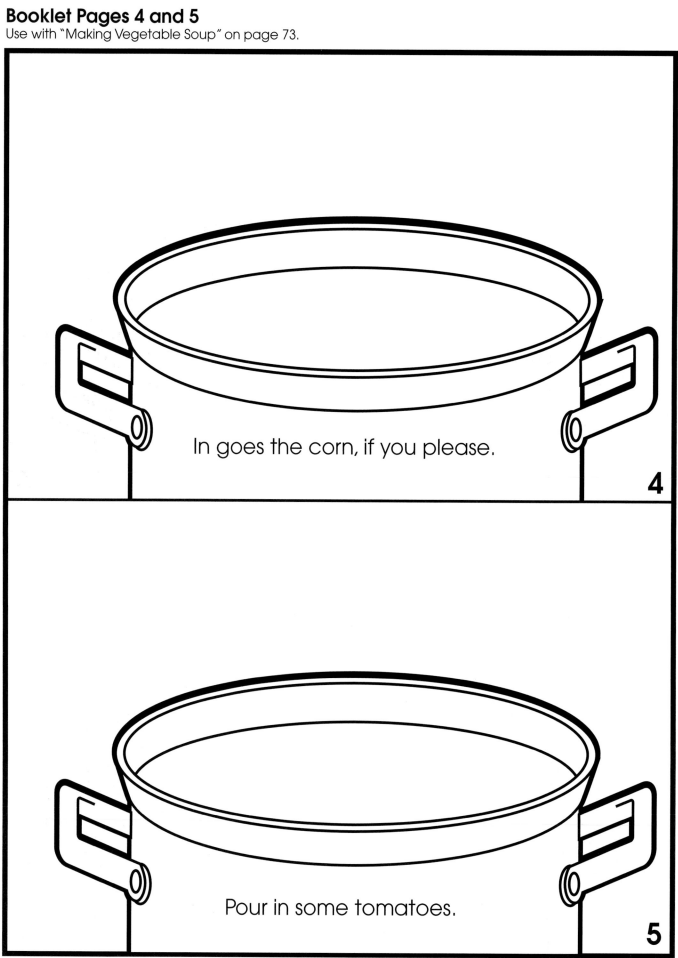

In goes the corn, if you please.

4

Pour in some tomatoes.

5

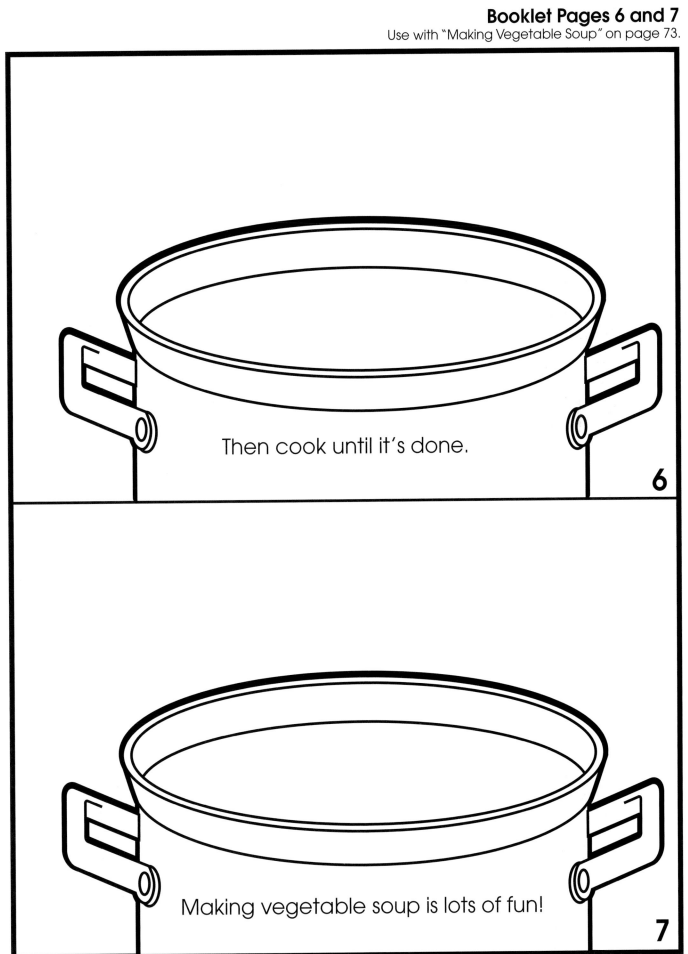

Then cook until it's done.

6

Making vegetable soup is lots of fun!

7

Soup Bowl Patterns
Use with "Chicken Soup Choices" on page 73.

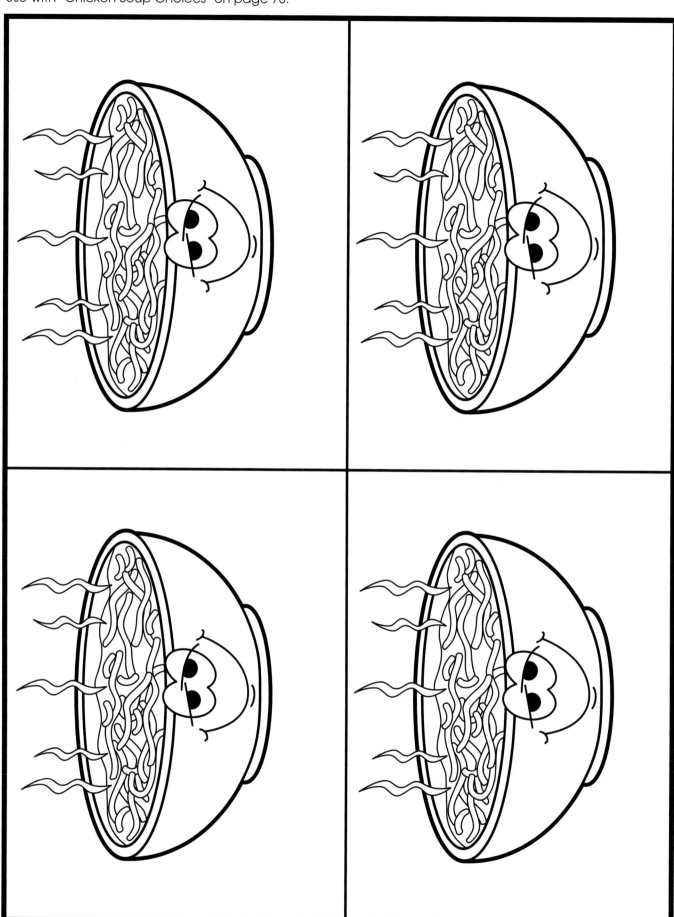

Sun and Shadows

When you run, it runs. When you jump, it jumps. And when you step into the shade, it hides! Try these super shadow activities in celebration of Groundhog Day...or any sunny day!

Have You Ever Seen a Shadow?

Give your youngsters an opportunity to see their own shadows in action by going outside on a sunny day to perform this shadowy song. Position each child in her own space so she can see her shadow. Then encourage each child to get her shadow moving by singing this song to the tune of "Did You Ever See a Lassie?"

Have you ever seen a shadow, a shadow, a shadow,
Have you ever seen a shadow
[Wave both of its hands]?
I'll [wave one hand] this way;
I'll [wave one hand] that way.
Have you ever seen a shadow
[Wave both of its hands]?

Repeat the song, substituting other action phrases, such as *wiggle both of its legs, stomp both of its feet, jump up and down,* and *twist side to side,* where indicated.

Observation Station

While your group is still outside enjoying the sun, invite your little shadow makers to observe their shadows in movement. Have each child stand with his back to the sun so he can see his shadow in front of him. Ask him to slowly turn around while observing his shadow for any changes in its length or location. Then discuss with each child the location of the sun in relation to his body and his shadow. Guide your youngsters to the conclusion that their bodies block the sun's light, which makes a shadow. How observant!

Opaque Images

Cast some light on why shadows appear with this simple demonstration activity. Select a volunteer assistant; then darken the classroom. Hold up your assistant's arm and ask students if they can see through it. Next, shine a flashlight beam on her arm to cast a shadow on the wall. Then ask students if the light shines through her arm. Explain to your youngsters that your assistant's arm blocked the light, which made a dark spot, or a shadow, on the wall. Conclude the demonstration by inviting your little shadow seekers to make some shadows of their own.

Did You Know?

When the sun shines on one side of the earth, it is daytime. At the same time, the other side of the earth is shadowed. The shadow creates the darkness of nighttime.

Shadow Makers

Now that your students understand that a light source paired with a light-blocking object creates a shadow, set up this enlightening center. Stock a center with a flashlight and small objects, such as building blocks, dolls, or school supplies. Demonstrate how to shine the flashlight beam on an object to make a shadow on a nearby wall. Invite each student to use the flashlight and objects to expose some shadowy images.

For a fun challenge, highlight students' investigational skills by adding clear and translucent objects to the center. Include items such as waxed paper, tissue paper, milk jugs, plastic cups and containers, and overhead transparencies. Encourage each child to predict which objects will cast distinct shadows; then have him test his predictions. After everyone has had a turn, discuss with students which objects made the most distinct shadows. Guide youngsters to the conclusion that the best shadow-making objects blocked the light. The waxed paper and tissue paper let some of the light shine through, so their shadows were not easily seen. The clear items let most of the light shine through them, resulting in slight shadows. Now that's illuminating!

Shadow Stumper

Screen your students' critical-thinking skills as they play this shadow guessing game. In advance, gather a variety of small, identifiable objects, such as pencils, scissors, and small toys. Place these objects in a paper bag to hide them from your students' view; then put the bag near your overhead projector. Form a screen around three sides of the projector by taping file folders around it as shown. To begin, take an object out of the bag and place it on the overhead projector. Then say the rhyme below, inserting a student's name.

Shadow-shape mystery, what could it be?
Tell me, [child's name], what do you see?

Repeat the rhyme as many times as desired, using a different object and naming a different student each time.

Step on It

This cooperative twist on a childhood favorite—shadow tag—is sure to encourage some enthusiastic shadow searching! While outside on a sunny day, choose two student volunteers to join hands and be It. Have the It team chase the rest of your group while chanting the rhyme below. When the It team steps on a player's shadow, he is caught. The player then joins the chasers by linking hands with them. As youngsters continue to play, the It team's chain will grow longer and longer! Play until everyone is caught, then start over with a new It team.

We see a shadow. Run, run, run!
Stepping on shadows is lots of fun!

The Word on Winter

What makes a chilly winter day more cozy than cuddling up with a good book? Share these winter tales to enchant your little book lovers with some interesting seasonal science ideas.

Time to Sleep

Written and Illustrated by Denise Fleming

Once Bear sniffs winter in the air, it doesn't take much time for all the animals in the forest to notice signs of the coming season. As you read the story, discuss the winter signs that the animals sense: a nip in the air, leaves turning different colors and falling, frost on the grass, shorter days, and full tummies! Then ask your students to suggest additional signs of winter that they have observed. Next, invite your youngsters to create this seasonal change art project to reinforce what they have learned. To prepare, fold a 12" x 18" sheet of dark blue construction paper into thirds for each child. If desired, divide the sections by drawing a black line along the two folds. Write "leaves change" at the top of the left section, "frost forms" at the top of the middle section, and "snow falls" at the top of the right section. To begin, have each child sponge-paint a yellow, an orange, and a red leaf in the first section. Next, ask each child to glue green paper strips of grass in the middle section and glue on clear glitter to represent frost. To complete the project, have each child glue cotton balls in the third section to represent snow. What lovely signs of the winter season!

When It Starts to Snow

Written by Phillis Gershator
Illustrated by Martin Matje

In winter when it starts to snow, what do the animals do and where do they go? When you share this seasonal story with your little ones, they'll have a wonderful time discovering how animals survive during winter! As you read and discuss the book, be sure to have your little story sleuths pay attention to what each animal does during winter storms! Then encourage your youngsters to recall the animals in the story and classify them into three groups. If desired, program a piece of chart paper to record their answers as shown. First, ask students to name the animals that spend winter sleeping or hibernating. Next, ask your youngsters to name the animals that need people to care for them in winter. Finally, ask your little ones which animals are able to take care of themselves outdoors during winter. Wrap up this cozy classification activity by allowing your youngsters to draw and color their favorite winterized animal!

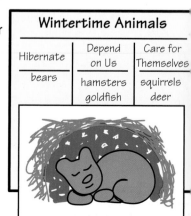

Wintertime Animals

Hibernate	Depend on Us	Care for Themselves
bears	hamsters goldfish	squirrels deer

When Winter Comes

Written and Photo-Illustrated by Robert Maass

Embrace your little ones with a wintry atmosphere as you read this realistic seasonal story. Encourage your students to discuss the outdoor winter attire in the photographs, especially the double-page spread of different hats in the book. Next, ask your youngsters to brainstorm reasons why they need to wear special hats when it is cold outside. Record their answers on a piece of hat-shaped chart paper titled "Why We Need Warm Winter Hats." Then challenge your students' inferential thinking skills with this activity, using a collection of seasonal hats (see suggestions below).

Place an assortment of hats in a large box. Next, ask a volunteer to remove one hat from the box and describe it. Then ask your youngsters to decide if it is the kind of hat worn when winter winds blow and storms are full of snow. Have your little ones separate the hats into seasonal stacks as each child analyzes a different one. Hats off to a job well done!

sun visor	canvas fishing hat	knit ski cap	detachable coat hood
straw hat	baseball cap	faux fur hat	wool cap with ear flaps

First Snow

Written and Illustrated by Kim Lewis

After reading the book to your little ones, prompt them to recall who discovered Sara's lost teddy bear—even though the snowstorm made it difficult to *see* very far. Ask your students what senses, other than sight, the dog may have used to find Sara's teddy bear. Then entice your youngsters to take on a similar rescue role as they search for little lost critters in make-believe snow! (Use the "snow-filled" sensory table described in "The Mittens I Wear in the Snow" on page 64.)

To prepare, secretly hide several small plush animals (including a white one) under the foam snow in the sensory table. Invite a small group of students to join you at the snow table. Challenge each child to close her eyes and use *only* her sense of smell to investigate and sniff out the critters hidden in the snow. Similarly, ask your students to use each of their other senses to search the snowdrift for the missing animals. Finally, encourage your youngsters to compare their searching skills to those of the faithful friend in the story. What keenly canine deductions!

The Jacket I Wear in the Snow

Written by Shirley Neitzel
Illustrated by Nancy Winslow Parker

Everyone knows to wear loose layers of clothes to stay warm in winter! After listening to the story, your little ones will warm up to science as they learn why loose layers are best for winter wear. In advance, collect two empty plastic peanut butter jars with lids and two 3½" x 42" strips of cotton cloth. To begin, wrap one piece of cloth around the first jar *tightly,* securing the end with masking tape. Next, wrap the other piece of cloth around the second jar *loosely.* Then fill both jars with very warm water and tighten the lids. Ask a volunteer to check each jar every ten minutes. Your students will be amazed to learn that the loosely wrapped jar stays warm longer than the tightly wrapped one. Explain to your youngsters that there is air trapped between the cloth and the jar, which keeps the heat inside the jar. The tightly wrapped cloth traps very little air next to the jar, so the heat escapes from it more quickly. Lead your little ones to conclude that wearing loose layers of clothing will trap heat next to their bodies. So when your little ones want to frolic in the nippy wintry weather and stay warm, remind them to wear loose layers of clothes!

Poppa's Itchy Christmas

Written by Angela Shelf Medearis
Illustrated by John Ward

Ahhh…nothing's better than ice skating on a pond amid a tranquil, wintry scene. But skating on a pond can be dangerous too. George thought the ice would hold him; after all, he stomped on the frozen pond's edge and it didn't break! After sharing this itchy, shivery story, ask your little ones to brainstorm reasons why the pond's ice was so thin in the middle while its edges seemed so solid. After discussing their ideas, invite each small group of youngsters to discover how a pond freezes. In advance, collect one individually sized pie tin for each child in the group. To begin, ask each child to slowly pour one-half cup of water into his pie tin; then put all the tins on a cookie sheet and place it in the freezer.

After an hour, remove the tins from the freezer. Encourage each child to discover whether the ice around the edge is stronger than the ice in the middle, and if he can break the center ice with his fingers. Explain to your youngsters that the water along the edge freezes first because the water there is shallow. The same is true in a pond because the pond's shallow water does not hold heat as well as the deeper water in the center. Also, the dirt and rocks at the pond's edge lose heat faster than the water does; making the shallow water freeze more rapidly. Cool!

Be Sweet to Your Heart

February is American Heart Month, so don't miss a beat in teaching your youngsters about this miraculous muscle!

Heartfelt Beat

Your little ones will really get a feel for what the heart is all about when they participate in this circle-time activity. As each child joins the circle, place a heart-shaped sticker on her shirt over her heart as shown. Be sure to put a sticker over your own heart too. Have each child place one hand on her heart sticker and sit quietly for about a minute. Then ask your students to describe what they feel as you write their responses on heart-shaped chart paper (keep for use with "We've Got the Beat!" at right). Lead your students to conclude that the thumping they feel is made by the beating of their hearts. Thumpity-thump!

This Is Why

The heart is a pump that moves blood throughout the body. When the heart pumps, it makes a beating sound. Before each beat, the heart fills up with blood; then it contracts to push the blood throughout the body. This creates a "lub-dub" sound, which we call a heartbeat.

We've Got the Beat!

Invite your students to sing the song below as they clap the rhythm of a heartbeat.

(sung to the tune of "Bingo")

This heart goes [thump-thump] all day long.
My heart's inside of me-o!
H-E-A-R-T! H-E-A-R-T! H-E-A-R-T!
My heart's inside of me-o!

Repeat the song several times, replacing "thump-thump" with a different phrase from the chart made in "Heartfelt Beat" above.

lub-dub
boom-boom
pit-pat

Healthy Hearts for All!

What is the most important muscle in your body? The heart, of course, because it pumps blood throughout the entire body. Discuss with your youngsters why a strong heart is healthy. Lead them to conclude that exercise can improve the strength of the heart, just as exercise strengthens all of the body's muscles.

To demonstrate the effect exercise has on heartbeat rate, ask each child to feel his heartbeat by placing his hand on his chest. Then encourage each child to clap a rhythm to imitate the sound of his resting heartbeat. Next, put on some lively music and invite your students to move vigorously for a few minutes. Stop the music and ask each child to again feel his heartbeat and clap a rhythm to imitate the faster rate. Encourage your students to compare the difference in the two heartbeat rates. Wrap up the activity by having the class brainstorm a chart of ideas for heart-strengthening activities they can do at home.

Do You Hear a Heartbeat?

Your little ones will be all ears when they take part in this heartbeat-detection session! To prepare, follow the directions below to make one heartbeat detector for every two students. To begin the activity, prompt youngsters to recall that each person has a heart and can feel her own heartbeat. Next, give each pair of students a heartbeat detector and invite them to take turns listening to their partner's heartbeat. Ask one child in each pair to place the open end of the cup over her partner's heart. Have the child place her ear firmly against the open end of the tube to hold the detector in place and then take her hands away from the cup. Encourage the group to be silent so that each listener can hear her partner's heartbeat. After both partners have taken a turn listening, have students switch partners to continue the heartbeat-detection process. Extend the activity by providing a stethoscope so that each child can detect the beat of her own heart. Lub-dub, lub-dub!

Materials needed for one heartbeat detector:

flexible plastic cup
bathroom tissue tube
duct tape
craft knife or scissors

Steps:
1. Use a craft knife or scissors to cut slashes in the bottom of the cup.
2. Push the tube through the bottom of the cup from the inside out.
3. Secure the tube to the cup with duct tape, making sure to cover all the cut edges.

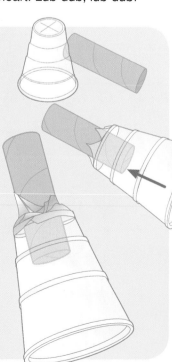

Building a Strong Heart

Here's a heart-healthy action rhyme that reinforces the importance of exercise to help the heart grow stronger.

My heart is right here.
It thump-thumps all day.
It beats when I work.
It beats when I play.
I can make my heart strong
With good exercise.
When I move and groove,
I'm being heart-wise.
So I promise to run
And play games each day,
So that I will be healthy
In every way!

Point to heart.
Pat chest two times.
Pretend to dig with a shovel.
Pretend to jump rope.
Flex biceps like a weight lifter.
Do jumping jacks.
Dance vigorously in place.
Point to head, nod, and smile.
Run in place.
Pretend to shoot baskets.
Stand up and smile.

Be Sweet to Your Heart

Wrap up these "hearty" learning experiences by inviting each child to make a "Be Sweet to Your Heart" booklet. To prepare, photocopy pages 88–91 onto white construction paper for each child. Instruct each child to cut out her cover and booklet pages. Read each page aloud; then help each child complete it according to the directions below. Later, help each child sequence the pages and then staple the booklet along the left side.

Cover: Write your name. Draw and color heart shapes around the booklet title.

Page 1: Color the heart red. Below it, write a phrase to describe the sound of a heartbeat. Draw and color your face and hair on the figure.

Page 2: At the top of the page, draw a picture of yourself working at home. At the bottom of the page, draw a picture of yourself playing outdoors.

Page 3: Draw yourself doing your favorite heart-smart activity.

Booklet Cover

Use with "Be Sweet to Your Heart" on page 87.

Be Sweet to Your Heart

by

____

1

Your heart is a muscle that's inside of you.

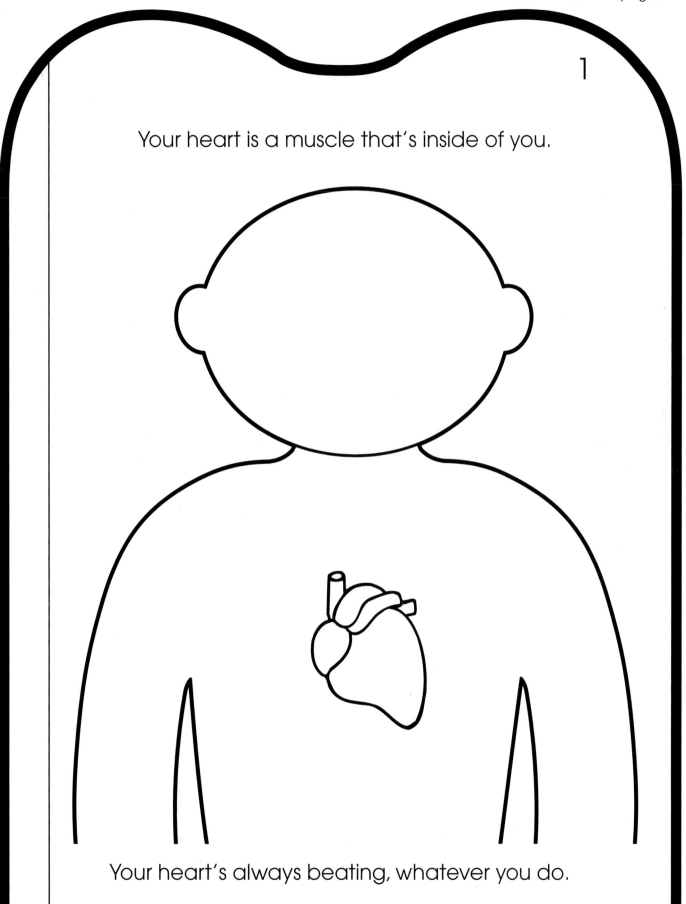

Your heart's always beating, whatever you do.

Booklet Page 2

Use with "Be Sweet to Your Heart" on page 87.

2

Your heart helps you work.

Your heart helps you play.

3

Be sweet to your heart each and every day!

The "Ice-sential" Facts

Ice is nice—especially for scientific discovery! Invite your little ones to check out some fun 'n' frosty facts as they learn about the properties of ice.

Freeze and Melt

Introduce your youngsters to the thrills and chills of ice with this easy experiment. To prepare, have youngsters help you fill enough ice cube trays with water to make one ice cube per child. Then freeze the trays overnight. The next day, have students help pop the cubes into a bowl. Invite each child to put an ice cube into a small paper cup. Have her observe the cube and discuss what happened to the water. Guide children to determine that placing the water in the freezer transformed it into ice. As you jot down their responses on chart paper, ask students to predict what will happen if the cubes are not returned to the freezer.

Direct students to place their cups on a table or windowsill. Later, have your little ones check the cups for changes. Ask your young scientists to describe their observations; then lead children to conclude that ice melts back into water when kept out of the freezer.

What Will Happen?

It will go away.
— Kath

Nothing.—Evan

It will melt.—Tra

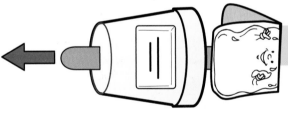

Pop-Up Puppets

These icy pop-up puppets will help reinforce your youngsters' concepts of freezing and melting. In advance, make a class supply of the puppet patterns on page 96, and cut a small slit in the bottom of a personalized eight-ounce foam cup for each child. To make a puppet, a child cuts out all the patterns and then glues the song patterns to opposite sides of the cup. He folds the ice cube/puddle pattern as indicated and sandwiches one end of a tongue depressor between the patterns and glues it shut. When the glue is dry, help the child insert the puppet into the slit in the cup to form a handle, as shown, making sure the patterns and text correspond.

Invite students to sing the song below while holding their puppets, turning their cups at the proper point in the song. When the song is finished, encourage children to slowly pull the handle to make the puddle disappear into the cup. Encourage youngsters to take their puppets home and sing this cool tune for family members.

I'm a little ice cube
From a tray.
I was just water yesterday.
Overnight I froze up
All the way.

Now watch me as I melt away!

(sung to the tune of "I'm a Little Teapot")

I'm a little ice cube
From a tray.
I was just water yesterday.
Overnight I froze up
All the way.
Now watch me as I melt away!

Please Pass the Salt

What happens when salt and ice meet? Try this easy experiment with your little investigators and you'll find out! Each child will need two small foam veggie trays (ask your grocer to donate unused trays) and two large ice cubes. You'll also need several shakers of salt for students to share. To begin, direct each child to place each ice cube on a separate foam tray. Have her shake some salt on one ice cube, leaving the other cube unsalted. Next, invite students to watch the ice cubes and compare what happens. They will be delighted to find that the salted ice cubes melt much more quickly than the unsalted cubes! Prompt a lively discussion by asking each child if both of her ice cubes are melting, if one is melting faster than the other, and what could be causing the ice to melt at such a fast rate.

This Is Why

Salt lowers the point at which water freezes. This causes the ice cube to melt. To prevent accidents, icy roads and sidewalks are often covered with salt. So if ice is on your winter sidewalk, say, "Please pass the salt!"

Five Little Ice Cubes

Here's a clever flannelboard song to reinforce the concept that salt melts ice. Begin by duplicating the ice cube patterns on page 96 and preparing them for use on a flannelboard. Now you're ready to sing!

(sung to the tune of "Five Little Ducks")

[Five] little ice cubes in a tray
Got popped out on a plate one day.
Salt sprinkled down and I heard one say,
"A sprinkle of salt makes me melt away!
Melt away! Melt away!
A sprinkle of salt makes me melt away!"

Repeat the song, subtracting one cube each time until all five little ice cubes have melted away.

Which Freezes First?

Continue your ice and salt explorations with this beautifully briny experiment. Fill one ten-ounce plastic cup with water. Add a tablespoon of salt to the water; then let each youngster take a turn stirring the contents. Have a student help you pour the salty water into an ice cube tray; then clip a clothespin marked with the letter *S* to the edge of the tray. Next, fill a second cup with plain water, making sure to point out that there is nothing but water in the cup. Have another student pour the plain water into a second ice cube tray. Put both trays into the freezer and then have youngsters help you check them a few times during the day. Your little ones will discover that plain water freezes in a shorter time than saltwater.

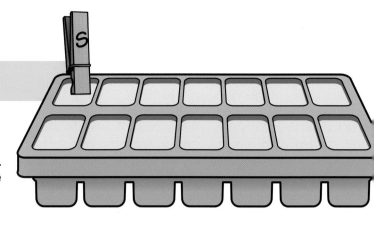

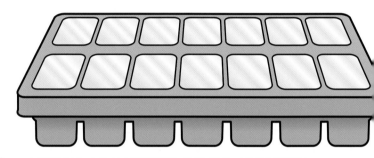

This Is Why
Plain water freezes at 32 degrees Fahrenheit. Adding salt to the water lowers the freezing point. The saltwater has to get colder to freeze, which takes longer.

Growing Ice

What grows when you freeze it? Water, of course! This easy icy cool activity is sure to grow some curiosity! All you need is a pitcher of water and a personalized, empty tomato-paste can for each child. To begin this small-group activity, help each student fill his can within a quarter inch of the top with water. Place the filled cans on a cookie sheet or tray and freeze overnight. The next day, give each child his can and encourage him to observe any changes that have occurred. Your youngsters will be astounded to discover that the ice looks as if it has grown! It is now higher than the original water line!

This Is Why
As water freezes, it *expands*, or grows larger.

> Abracadabra!
> Zim! Zam! Zing!
> I'll pull out the ice cube
> with only my string!

Abracadabra...Freeze!

Invite your youngsters to perform this amazing trick to showcase the magic of science. For each child, gather a small cup of water, an ice cube, a "magic wand" (a pencil), and an eight-inch length of string or yarn. You'll also need a few shakers of salt for students to share. Have each child place an ice cube in her cup of water. Challenge each youngster to try to use only her string to remove the ice cube from the cup. Then have each child dip one end of the string in the water and place it on top of her ice cube. Have her sprinkle a bit of salt on top of the string and the ice cube. Wait about a minute. While waiting, have each student wave her magic wand over the cup and say the magic words shown.

Next, direct each child to pull her string. Youngsters will discover that they are able to lift the ice cubes out of the water using only the strings! Encourage students to brainstorm why the string stuck to the ice. Was it the magic wand or the magic words? Or was it the salt? Try the experiment again without the magic wand or magic words.

This Is Why

The salt melted part of the ice cube, but the rest of it remained frozen. Waiting for a minute allowed the melted water to refreeze around the string.

Puppet Patterns
Use with "Pop-Up Puppets" on page 92.

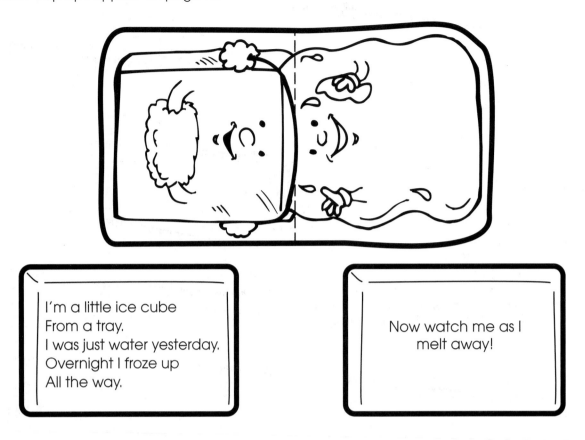

I'm a little ice cube
From a tray.
I was just water yesterday.
Overnight I froze up
All the way.

Now watch me as I
melt away!

Ice Cube Patterns
Use with "Five Little Ice Cubes" on page 93.

Insulation Station

Warm up your classroom with these simple insulation activities that trap warm air—or cold air!

Trapping Heat

Mittens keep little fingers warm on a frosty day, but where does the warmth come from? Begin your study of insulation with this two-step demonstration and let your youngsters discover how mittens keep their fingers warm.

Step 1: Place a plastic-backed thermometer outside for five minutes. Then assist several student volunteers in checking the thermometer. Record the observed temperature on a piece of chart paper. Next, slip the thermometer inside a mitten or glove and place it outdoors where it will not be disturbed. After about an hour, help a second set of student volunteers check and record the temperature reading of the thermometer. Discuss the results with your students; they'll be surprised to discover that the temperature is still the same! So if the mitten has no heat inside, what makes it warm?

Step 2: Assist a student volunteer in checking and recording the temperature reading from another plastic-backed thermometer to establish a baseline. Slip the thermometer into a mitten or glove; then help a student carefully put the mitten on with the thermometer inside. Have him sit quietly for about five minutes and then help him recheck the temperature. Your students will discover that the temperature changed. Encourage children to brainstorm reasons why the temperature was different. After discussing student ideas, lead your little ones to conclude that the heat could not have been in the mitten, but was from the student's body. Wow! Trapping heat is neat!

This Is Why

The mitten in the experiment provided a heat trap (an insulator), which prevented the student's body heat from escaping.

It's a Wrap!

If mittens and gloves keep heat from escaping, do woolen scarves work the same way? Try this nifty experiment to find out. In advance, gather two large plastic cups, two thermometers, and a piece of wool fabric (or a wool scarf) for a small-group experiment. You'll also need a pitcher of very warm (but not hot) water. Begin by pouring about two inches of water into each cup. Then direct a child to carefully place a thermometer in each cup. Assist a group of students in reading the thermometers and confirming that the water in both cups is the same temperature. Next, help a student volunteer gently wrap a woolen scarf around one cup. Encourage your group to watch the thermometers for any changes. Ask students to observe which cup of water cools more quickly. Then invite each child to explain why one cup cools faster than the other. After each student has shared, explain that the cup wrapped with the scarf stayed warmer because the water's heat was trapped by the scarf. Your mother was right—woolies keep you warmer!

Which One Stays Cooler?

Now that your students are warmed up, help them discover the cool side of insulation with this simple demonstration! To prepare, obtain a foam soda can holder. Chill two cans of soda and then have your little ones handle both cans to verify that they are cold. Next, initiate a discussion about what would happen to the temperature of the cans if they were left on a table for an hour. Then show your youngsters the foam can holder and have them predict what might happen if it were placed on one of the cans. After discussing student ideas, sing the first verse of the song below with your class. At the appropriate spot in the song, slip the can holder onto one of the cans. Let both soda cans sit undisturbed for about an hour. Then gather your students and take the soda can out of the holder. So that each child can discover which can feels cooler, separately pass around both cans. Place the can holder with the appropriate can and then put both cans in front of your students. Next, sing the second verse of the song and have students point to the cooler can at the appropriate time. Encourage your young thinkers to brainstorm reasons why the can in the holder stayed cooler. Culminate the activity by serving each child a small cup of chilled soda in an insulated cup.

(sung to the tune of "My Bonnie Lies Over the Ocean")

Verse 1
Let's find out which can stays cooler.
Let's leave them both right here and see.
Let's put a can holder on this one
And just let the other one be.
Which one, which one,
Oh, which one stays cooler?
We'll see, we'll see!
Which one, which one,
Oh, which one stays cooler? We'll see!

Verse 2
We put a can holder on this one.
We just let the other one be.
We let them both sit for an hour,
And this one is cooler to me.
This one, this one,
Oh, this one is cooler to me, to me!
This one, this one,
Oh, this one is cooler to me!

This Is Why!

Warm air is blocked from the chilled can of soda by the can holder, which acts as an insulator. The can holder will keep the soda cool for a while, but not forever. Heat will ultimately pass through the can holder (and through the exposed portion of the can), causing the soda to become warm.

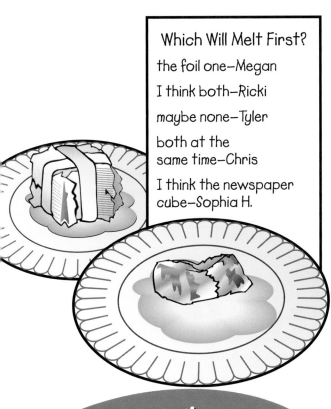

Which Will Melt First?

the foil one—Megan

I think both—Ricki

maybe none—Tyler

both at the
same time—Chris

I think the newspaper
cube—Sophia H.

The Winning Ice Cube Is...

How do you keep an ice cube from melting? Insulate it, of course! Have your young scientists use their predicting and observation skills to discover which common materials make good insulators with this ice cube race. Working with one small group at a time, give each child two same-size ice cubes, two personalized paper plates, one 4" x 4" square of aluminum foil, a newspaper page, and two rubber bands. Direct each child to wrap one ice cube in foil. Have her wrap the other ice cube in newspaper; then help her secure the newspaper with her rubber bands. Next, have her place the wrapped ice cubes on separate plates. As you record student responses on chart paper, ask each child to predict which material will better insulate the ice and therefore win the race. Put the plates in an undisturbed area and let the ice cubes "race" for an hour; then have students inspect their plates to see how much water each contains. Discuss which ice cube melted more and which melted less. Guide students to determine that the newspaper-wrapped ice cube won the race because it lasted longer than the foil-wrapped cube. Compare the race results to the list of predictions and then extend this activity by inviting your group to test other common items (socks, plastic wrap, paper towels, napkins, plastic containers, waxed paper, etc.) to find out how well they insulate. This is one race that's all wrapped up!

This Is Why

Newspaper is made of fibers that contain small air pockets. The air pockets trapped the heat from the classroom, helping the ice cube stay frozen. Foil conducts heat more readily than newspaper, so the room's heat reaches the ice cube faster. Therefore, newspaper makes a better insulator than foil!

You've Got to Have Some Insulation

Cozy up and sing this little ditty to reinforce what your little ones have already learned about insulation!

*(sung to the tune of
"I've Been Working on the Railroad")*

You've got to have some insulation
To keep things hot or cold!
You've got to have some insulation
So temperatures will hold!
Let your hands stay warm in mittens
And keep your drink real cold!
You've got to have some insulation
To keep things hot or cold!

Insulation Fans

There are many different kinds of insulation, but which materials best trap heat to keep us warm? Set up this chilling center activity and invite your little ones to find out. To prepare, stock a center with a cooler full of ice water and several different insulation mitts (see "How to Make an Insulation Mitt" below). Show students each mitt and discuss the insulation material it contains. Ask them to predict which mitts will keep their hands warm; then jot their responses on a chart. Then invite each little scientist to visit the center and test each mitt. Have him slip his hand into a mitt and plunge it into the icy water, keeping the top of the mitt above the water. After each child has had an opportunity to test the mitts, chart and discuss the results. So which materials protected little hands from the cold?

How to Make an Insulation Mitt

Step 1: Fill a gallon-size resealable plastic freezer bag with one of the materials listed below.

Step 2: Turn a quart-size resealable plastic freezer bag inside out; then place it inside the larger bag to form the mitt.

Step 3: Tape the mitt into place with duct tape.

Step 4: Seal the larger bag on either side of the smaller bag and reinforce the seal with duct tape.

Suggested materials:

shredded newspaper	waxed paper	kitchen towels
packing peanuts	craft batting	rice
aluminum foil	cotton balls	sand
craft feathers	wood chips/sawdust	
bubble wrap		
vegetable shortening		

Step 1

Step 2

Step 3

Step 4

Spring

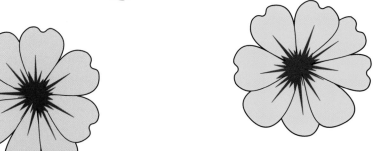

Investigating Rain

It's raining, it's pouring...and scientific knowledge will be soaring when you invite your students to spend some time investigating rain!

Who Likes Rain?

How many of your little ones delight in the sight of a rainy-day downpour? Find out with this graphing activity. To prepare, create a two-column graph labeled as shown. Then ask your youngsters whether they like or dislike rain. After discussing students' feelings, give each child a photocopied raindrop pattern from page 107. If the child likes rain, have her draw a smile on her raindrop. If she does not like rain, have her draw a frown. Ask each child to write her name on the line, cut out her raindrop, and post it on the graph. Then take a few minutes to discuss the results. Once you've completed the activities in this unit, poll students and graph their attitudes a second time. You may find that those who once found rain to be a pain have changed their minds!

Simulating Rain

Even if the forecast is for clear skies with not a shower in sight, your youngsters can simulate a rainstorm right inside the classroom! To begin this rhythmic rain simulation, have students sit cross-legged on the floor in a circle. Recite each stanza of the following chant, prompting students to perform the accompanying motion. Recite the first stanza in a whisper; then gradually increase the volume of your voice with each stanza. To finish off the faux rain shower, repeat the chant and sounds for each stanza in reverse order. There's nothing like the rhythmical sounds of a rainy day!

Rain, rain, rain, rain,
Whispering on the windowpane.
Rub hands together.

Rain, rain, rain, rain,
Tapping on the windowpane.
Snap fingers.

Rain, rain, rain, rain,
Slapping on the windowpane.
Slap thighs with hands.

Rain, rain, rain, rain,
Drumming on the windowpane.
Slap floor with hands.

Let's Make Rain Sticks!

Introduce your youngsters to another way to simulate the sound of rain when you make rain sticks together in a small-group setting. To make a rain stick, first push 14 large (1½-inch) metal brads into a paper towel tube to form a random pattern along the entire length of the tube. Use clear packing tape to secure a cardboard circle (1½ inches in diameter) to one end of the tube. Next, place two to three tablespoons of *one* of the materials from the list below inside the tube. Then use more clear packing tape to secure another cardboard circle to the open end of the tube. Finish the rain stick by wrapping the tube with gift wrap or construction paper.

To use the rain stick, grasp each end lightly and hold the tube perpendicular to the floor. When you hear that all the material inside has "rained" to the lower end of the tube, flip the rain stick and begin the shower of sound all over again!

Rain stick fillers:

Rice Krispies cereal	dried beans or peas	elbow macaroni	sequins
Cheerios cereal	small metal washers	small plastic beads	aquarium gravel

Rain Stick Pairs

Each of the rain sticks your youngsters create for the previous activity will have its own unique sound because of the variety of fillers and the differences in the brad patterns. Make some extra rain sticks with similar brad patterns and matching materials to test your youngsters' auditory skills. Use the directions in "Let's Make Rain Sticks!" to prepare two rain sticks with elbow macaroni, two with aquarium gravel, two with Rice Krispies cereal, and two with sequins. Then gather a small group of students and invite them to play with the rain sticks for a few minutes. Encourage them to discuss the sounds they hear. Then challenge them to pair up the rain sticks that have the same sounds. After some trial and error and a bit of discussion, your little sound scientists should be able to make matches that are as right as rain!

Rain Indications

How can you tell that it's rained even if you haven't seen the rain falling? Pursue this question by asking students to imagine they have gone to bed one evening while the skies are clear. Upon waking in the morning, what would they see outside to tell them that it had rained during the night? Encourage a discussion; then write your youngsters' ideas on chart paper. Later, use the students' suggestions in the song below.

How Can You Tell It Has Rained?

The streets are wet.
The grass is wet.
You see puddles.
The slide is wet.
There are raindrops on the window.

The Rain Came Down

Teach your young scientists this splashy song to reinforce the ideas discussed in "Rain Indications" (above). Sing this song on a rainy spring day; then go outside for a post-rain puddle hunt!

(sung to the tune of "Buffalo Gals")

How do we know that it rained in the night,
Rained in the night, rained in the night?
How do we know that it rained in the night?
We see that [the streets are wet]!

Substitute other student suggestions from the chart for the underlined phrase.

The Disappearing Puddle

Have your youngsters noticed that—little by little—even the biggest rain puddles eventually disappear? Here's an easy way to visually record the shrinkage of a puddle. To begin, take your class outdoors in the morning after a rain. Work together to find a big puddle on a paved surface. Use chalk to draw a line on the pavement just outside the perimeter of the puddle. Return to the puddle periodically to draw a new line around it. (Depending on the weather and the location of your puddle, you may need to return every hour or over the course of a day or two.) Encourage students to compare the old and new lines. Has the puddle changed in size? Continue to record the puddle's size until it disappears. Then talk about what has happened to the water. Share the information in "This Is Why" with your young puddle experts!

This Is Why

When water puddles on a surface like a sidewalk or pavement, the heat of the sun slowly causes the liquid water to change into *water vapor*, which is a gas. The water vapor then rises into the air. This process is called *evaporation*. Water evaporates slowly, so the puddle shrinks over time.

Which Puddle Persists?

How can you come up with puddles to study when there's not a rain shower in sight? Make some yourself! In advance, find areas outdoors suitable for making several puddles. You'll need to find a spot in the dirt, in the sand, on the grass, on a sidewalk, and on blacktop, if possible. Try to find five locations fairly close together. Next, prepare a chart with a column for each area where you plan to place a puddle.

Take your youngsters outdoors. Have student volunteers pour buckets of water on each of your five selected surfaces to create five puddles. (Pour an equal amount of water on each surface.) Once the puddles are made, ask students to predict which puddle of water will last the longest. To record the life span of each puddle, have students check them periodically (depending upon your weather). Record students' findings on the chart. Which puddle is the most persistent?

This Is Why

The more *absorbent* the surface, the shorter the life span of the puddle. Puddles disappear quickly on absorbent surfaces such as soil and sand because the water simply soaks in.

time	sand	dirt	blacktop	sidewalk	grass
10:00	The puddle is gone already.	This puddle is much smaller.	This is the biggest puddle.	This puddle is still big.	This puddle is almost gone.
11:30		This puddle is gone now.	This puddle got smaller.	This puddle is smaller.	This puddle is gone now.
1:00			This puddle got a little smaller.	This one is almost gone.	
2:00			Still here!	There's just a tiny bit left!	

Puddle Comparisons

Explore puddles further with this small-group activity at your sand table. Direct students to dig two depressions in the sand to create small basins for puddles. Lay a paper towel inside one basin; lay a piece of plastic wrap inside the other. Pour some water into each basin to make a puddle, being sure to keep the water level below the edge of the liner. Have students observe the puddles and describe what happens. Why do they think the puddle lined with the paper towel disappeared? Where did the water go?

Extend this absorbing experiment by inviting students to test other materials as puddle liners, such as waxed paper, muslin, a plastic bag, aluminum foil, and newsprint. Add a chart, labeled as shown, to the area. Have students cut and glue samples of the puddle-lining materials to the chart to display their findings.

This Is Why

The puddle lined with plastic wrap lasts longer because the plastic wrap blocks the absorption of the water into the sand. The paper towel absorbs the water and allows it to soak into the sand quickly.

Good Puddle Liners waxed paper plastic bag aluminum foil

Not-So-Good Puddle Liners muslin newsprint

Rain Gets Things Wet!

Invite your weather-savvy students to create these rain-themed booklets. To prepare, duplicate the booklet cover and pages on pages 108–110 on white paper for each child. Read through the directions below and gather the necessary materials. (For younger students, you may wish to precut the circle on page 5 of the booklet.) Have each child cut out his cover and pages before illustrating them as directed below. Help each child complete his booklet by stacking the cover and pages in order and stapling them together along the left side.

Cover: Color the cloud gray. Glue blue paper strips to the bottom of the cloud to resemble rain. Write your name on the line.

Page 1: Color the windowpanes gray. Make dots on each pane with blue glitter glue.

Page 2: Color the cloud gray. Draw a house under the cloud. Glue pieces of blue yarn to the bottom of the cloud to resemble rain.

Page 3: Color the cloud gray. Draw green grass at the bottom of the page. Use a thin paintbrush to paint blue rain below the cloud.

Page 4: Color the cloud gray. Draw something that gets wet when it rains. Write the word on the blank. Use a blue marker to draw rain.

Page 5: Color the umbrella. Cut out the circle on the page. Tape a photocopy of your school photo to the back of the page so that your face shows through the opening. Use blue glitter glue to draw rain.

Singin' of the Rain

Reinforce the theme of the booklet with a song you *won't* want to save for a rainy day! To add additional verses, encourage students to suggest vocabulary from their booklets to replace the underlined word.

(sung to the tune of "If You're Happy and You Know It")

Oh, do you know what happens when it rains? *Clap twice.*
Oh, do you know what happens when it rains? *Clap twice.*
When it rains, the [trees] get wet. Oh yes! It's true, you bet!
Yes, that is just what happens when it rains! *Clap twice.*

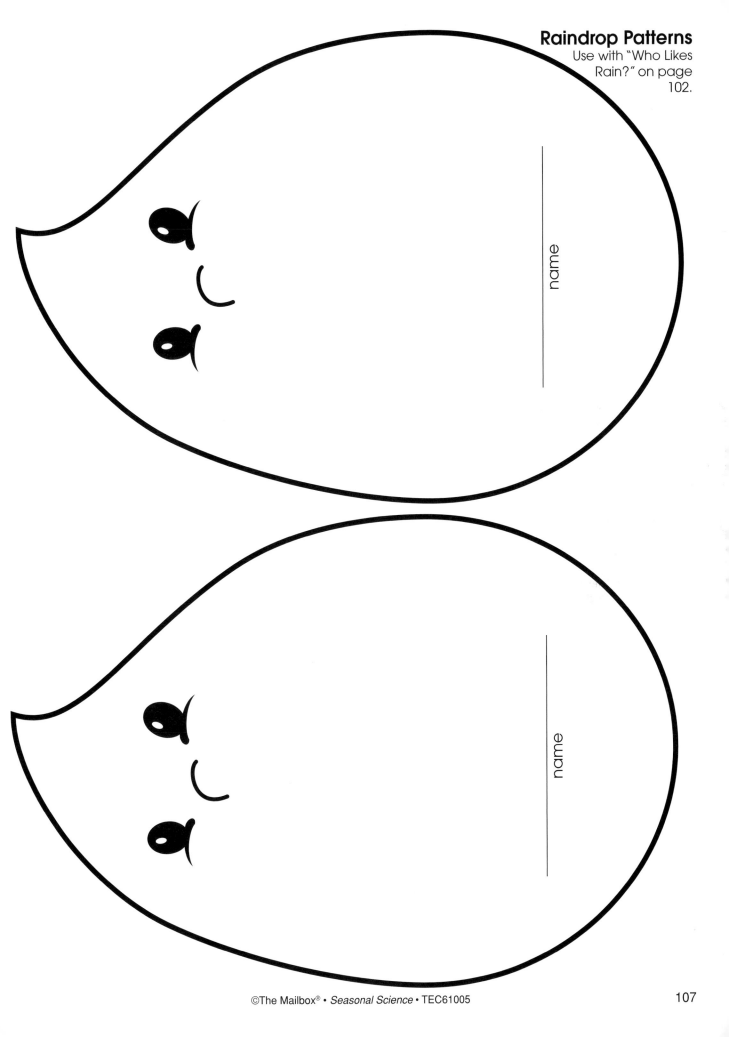

name

name

Rain Gets Things Wet!

by _____

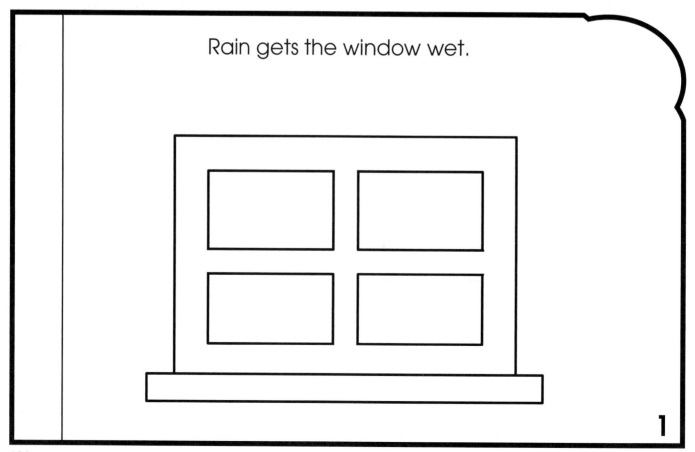

Rain gets the window wet.

1

Rain gets the house wet.

2

Rain gets the grass wet.

3

Rain gets the _____ wet.

4

But it doesn't get me wet!

5

Little Sprouts

Your little ones will be sprouting up lots of scientific knowledge as they explore and discover what seeds, edible bulbs, flowering bulbs, and vegetable tops have in common!

Interesting Edibles

Give your little ones a taste of fun as they investigate sprouts! To prepare, ask parents to donate different types of edible sprouts from your local grocery or health food store. Invite each child to put a spoonful of sprouts on a small paper plate; then have him examine his sprouts. Tell students that the sprouts before them are edible. After discussing student observations, encourage your youngsters to taste several sprouts. Mmm, interesting!

No Soil or Sunlight Needed!

Now that your little ones have observed sprouts, they will be eager to grow their own! Have parents donate alfalfa seeds, mustard seeds, or dried chickpeas from your local grocery or health food store. Put the seeds in a shallow pan of water and soak them overnight; then rinse the seeds in a colander. Have each student put a spoonful of seeds in a personalized clear plastic cup and then use a rubber band to secure a 5" x 5" muslin square to the top. Have students predict what will happen to the seeds without soil and sunlight. Then have students set their cups in a warm, dark place. Daily, remind each student to gently pour water through the muslin of her cup, swirl the seeds around in the water, and then pour the water out through the muslin. In approximately three days, your youngsters will be delighted to see that their seeds have sprouted without soil or sunlight. Vary this activity with lentils, mung beans, or cress seeds. Anyone for sprouts?

This Is Why
Seeds can sprout, or germinate, without direct sunlight or nutrients from the soil because each seed has its own food that allows it to sprout and begin growing in moist, warm conditions.

Cozy or Chilly?

Your youngsters will find out if seeds sprout in warm or cool temperatures with this scientific experiment. In advance, ask your local grocery store to donate two foam meat trays. Line each tray with a layer of wet cotton balls. Spread two tablespoons of alfalfa seeds evenly on each tray. Have your students predict how warm or cool temperatures will affect the seeds. Then place one tray in a sunny area and the other tray in a refrigerator. After several days, your students will notice that the seeds getting warmth from the sun are sprouting. Ask them to predict what the seeds in the refrigerator look like. Then have your little ones compare the trays. Seeds like it warm!

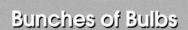

Bunches of Bulbs

Reinforce observation skills with this small-group activity. To prepare, have parents donate edible bulbs, such as white onions, yellow onions, red onions, small pearl onions, green onions (scallions), garlic, and leeks. When all the bulbs have arrived, put them on a table and invite each student in a small group to observe and compare the bulbs. After examining the bulbs' colors, sizes, shapes, and textures, challenge them to sort the bulbs into groups. Explain to your young learners that these particular bulbs can be eaten just as sprouts can be eaten, but that some bulbs are poisonous. Encourage your little ones to ask their parents for tastes of edible bulbs at home!

An Inside Study of Onions

Have your little scientists investigate the insides of onions and then make onion prints! Before the activity, cut a yellow, white, and red onion in half horizontally. Enclose each onion half in a resealable plastic bag. To begin the activity, have each child study and compare the inside moist layers with the outer papery layers of each onion half. Next, remove each onion from its bag and insert a fork for a handle as shown. Invite each child to don a pair of safety glasses, dip each type of onion into a shallow pan of tempera paint, and then make prints on a sheet of construction paper. Lead students to the conclusion that onions can be different sizes and shapes. As a finishing touch, display these colorful prints around your room.

Did You Know?

A bulb is a thick, fleshy plant bud under the soil that stores food for the plant. Not all bulbs are edible; most flowering bulbs are poisonous.

Sprouting Bulbs

Your little ones will be amazed to discover that edible bulbs sprout too! In advance, have parents donate a class supply of garlic bulbs. Personalize an eight-ounce clear plastic cup for each child. Cut a class supply of foam circles to fit inside the cups as shown. Next, cut an X in the center of each circle, just large enough for a garlic clove to be inserted without falling out. Have a small group of students examine the garlic heads, compare them with onions, and then break the garlic heads apart to reveal individual cloves. Initiate a discussion about whether the cloves are alive or not. Then use the directions below to have your students complete the experiment. Roots and sprouts will appear in approximately three days. Use the newly sprouted cloves in "Sprout Portraits" below.

Directions:

1. Peel the papery layer from a garlic clove.
2. Gently push your clove, pointed end up, into the X in a foam circle.
3. Fill your cup halfway with water. Put the circle in your cup. Make sure that the bottom of the clove is in the water.
4. Set your cup near a sunny window, and check each day for any changes.
5. Add water as needed to keep the bottom of the clove wet.

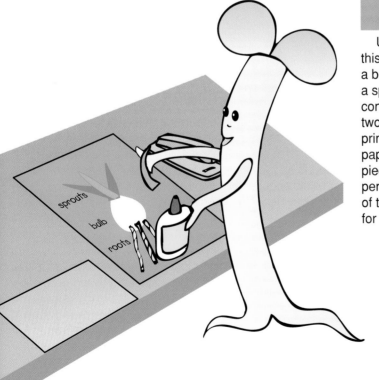

Sprout Portraits

Use the sprouts from "Sprouting Bulbs" as models for this scientific diagram activity. To make one diagram, use a bulb-shaped sponge and white tempera paint to make a sponge print in the center of a 6" x 9" sheet of colored construction paper. When the paint is dry, glue several two-inch lengths of white yarn to the bottom of the bulb print to resemble roots. Next, glue several green tissue paper sprouts to the top of the bulb print. Staple a 4" x 6" piece of waxed paper across the bottom portion of the paper to represent water; then have students label the parts of their bulbs as shown. Display these sprouting portraits for all to see!

Did You Know?
A head of garlic is a bulb. Each small clove is a separate bulb. Garlic and onions are examples of edible bulbs.

Bulbs A-bloomin'!

Your little ones will bloom with enthusiasm as they learn about inedible bulbs that sprout flowers! In advance, purchase an inexpensive pot of blooming daffodils, tulips, or hyacinths. Have your students describe the plant parts. Then have them brainstorm what might be underneath the soil. Remove two of the flowers with their bulbs intact. Split one bulb in half lengthwise; then invite students to examine both bulbs.

If you already have small spring flowering bulbs such as paperwhites or hyacinths, extend your inedible bulb study by forcing the bulbs to bloom. Place the bulbs in a paper bag and store them in the refrigerator for four to six weeks. To sprout a chilled bulb, set it in the mouth of a narrow, water-filled, clear plastic jar so that only the rounded base of the bulb is submerged. Encourage your youngsters to discuss the daily changes that they observe. Grow, flowers, grow!

Sprouting Is Tops!

Not only seeds and bulbs sprout! Demonstrate to your little ones that some vegetable tops will sprout and grow if sunlight and water are provided. To prepare for this activity, remove the greens from two red beets and two carrots; then cut them two inches down from their crowns. Fill two shallow pans with gravel and water. Put a carrot and a beet, cut side down, into each pan. Place one pan near a warm, sunny window and the other in a cool, dark place. Make sure to water the vegetable tops daily. When the window vegetables have sprouted leaves (approximately three to six days), compare the two pans. Lead your little scientists to conclude that vegetable tops need a supply of bright, warm light to grow!

Sprouts All About

Culminate this unit by having your little learners make these smashing sprout booklets. In advance, make a class supply of pages 115 and 116 on white construction paper; then cut the pages apart. Gather the necessary supplies and then use the suggestions below to help each student complete a booklet. Have each child sequence her pages and staple them behind the cover on the left-hand side. Read all about sprouts!

Cover: Print your name on the line. Draw and then color several seeds and bulbs.
Page 1: Glue on a two-inch square of paper towel. Use a cotton swab to paint seeds on the towel. Use a green marker to draw a sprout growing from each seed.
Page 2: Cut out the cup pattern and glue it to the page. Use a blue crayon to color water in the cup. Glue on pieces of string for roots. Draw a sprout.
Page 3: Make an orange carrot-top print in the dish. Draw green leaves sprouting from the carrot top.
Page 4: Color the flower pattern red or blue and then cut it out. Glue the flower stem where indicated so that it extends above the top of the page. Then fold the flower down. Use a gray or black washable ink pad to make fingerprints in the pan to resemble gravel.

What Will Sprout?

by _____

Seeds
and beans
will sprout.

1

Garlic
will sprout too.

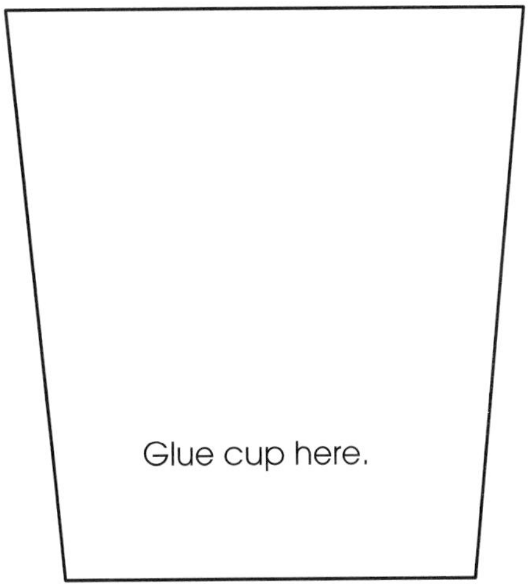

Glue cup here.

2

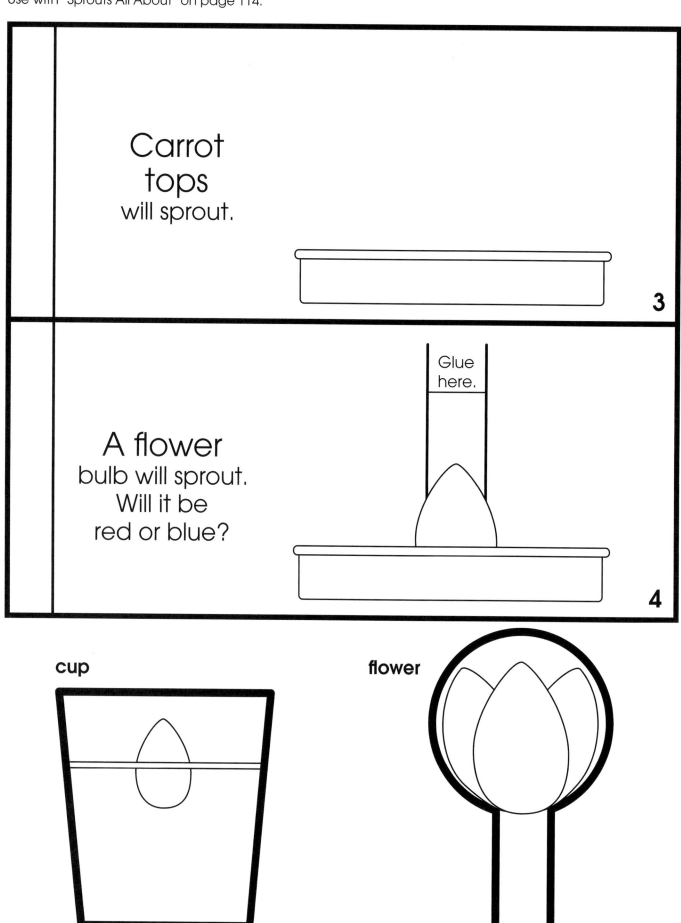

Carrot
tops
will sprout.

3

A flower
bulb will sprout.
Will it be
red or blue?

Glue
here.

4

cup

flower

Give Me Five for Snacktime!

Focus your scientific studies on the five senses with these mouthwatering activities!

Calling All Senses!

Your little ones will be in touch with their senses as they investigate this surprise snack! In advance, duplicate the recording sheet on page 120 for each student. Put a scoop of cereal into a paper lunch bag for each child. To begin the activity, sing the song below with a small group of students. Shake the bag, having students silently guess what is inside by listening. Next, give each child a recording sheet; then have her draw a picture of her guess in the first box. Sing the song again, substituting *smelling* for the underlined words. Following the same sensory process, have each child sniff her bag and then draw a picture of her guess. Continue in this manner until all five sensory guesses have been recorded. Discovery has never been so much fun!

(sung to the tune of "Are You Sleeping?")

Can you guess? Can you guess?
What's inside? What's inside?
Do you know by [listening]?
Do you know by [listening]?
What's inside? What's inside?

All Eyes on Color!

This center idea will have your little scientists seeing colors in a new way! In advance, stock a center with empty egg cartons and several small bowls of Froot Loops cereal. (Be sure to have extras nearby for munching.) When a child visits this center, have him sort a bowl of cereal by placing each different color into a separate carton compartment. Next, have him use his sense of sight to identify the dark and light colors. Then have him count the cereal pieces in each carton compartment. After he compares each one, have the student put the cereal pieces back in the bowl. Give a high five for eyes!

This Is Why

The cereal pieces could be sorted by color because *cones* in the eye tell the brain what color they are. *Rods* detect only black and white.

Tasty Textures

This discovery activity will introduce your little ones to a variety of tempting textures! In advance, have parents donate a large container of vanilla yogurt, a box of saltine crackers, a box of chewy granola bars, small paper plates, and plastic spoons. Duplicate and then cut apart the response sheets on page 121 to make a class supply. To begin the activity, have students brainstorm crunchy, soft, and chewy foods; record their responses on a piece of chart paper. At snacktime, have each child sample the foods; then have her compare their textures. Give each child a response sheet; then help her record her response. Next, instruct the child to draw a food with her favorite texture in the bubble. Then have her draw a picture of herself (or glue a small photo) in the rectangle. Display the completed projects on a bulletin board. Then use the display as a discussion guide to determine the class's favorite textures. No doubt about it—textures are terrific!

Each kind of food is such a treat.
But a ___chewy___ ___granola bar___ is what I like to eat!
     (texture)   (food)

Sweet or Sour?

Involve your students in some sweet, sour, salty, and bitter taste testing! In advance, put each of the following in a separate bowl: sugar, salt, unsweetened lemonade drink powder, and unsweetened cocoa. Program an 8½" x 11" sheet of paper to resemble the tasting mat shown; then copy it to make a class supply. Give each student a mat, and put a small amount of one ingredient in the first section. Ask each child to examine the ingredient and predict the flavor. Then invite him to sprinkle a small pinch of the ingredient on his tongue and identify its taste as sweet, sour, salty, or bitter. Continue the activity until all four ingredients have been tried. Discuss students' predictions and their results. Your budding scientists will be amazed at what taste buds can do!

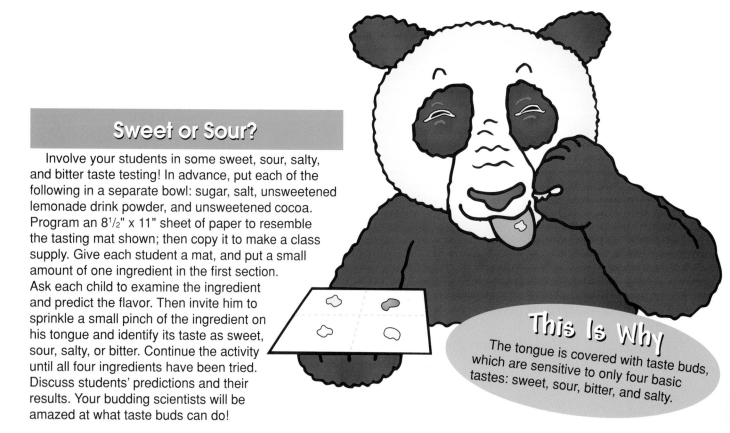

This Is Why
The tongue is covered with taste buds, which are sensitive to only four basic tastes: sweet, sour, bitter, and salty.

118

Noisy Nibblers

Combine the senses of hearing and taste and what do you get? Lots of delicious crunching and munching! Gather your students and review the list of crunchy foods generated in "Tasty Textures" on page 118. Then give each child a thin apple slice. On the count of three, have each child take a bite out of his slice. Invite students to discuss what kinds of sounds they heard (crunching, popping, snapping, etc.). Next, sing the song below with your students, each time substituting a different crunchy food in place of the underlined word. Crunch, crunch!

(sung to the tune of "Pop! Goes the Weasel")

Did you know that some foods crunch?
You'll hear them loud and clear.
Bite [an apple]—crunch, crunch, crunch!
Music to my ears!

"Sense-ational" Snacks

Culminate this unit with a flavorful snack that combines all five senses. To make one snack portion, have each child put five of each ingredient listed below into a resealable plastic bag. Have her seal the bag and then shake it gently to listen to the sound. Have her use her sense of sight to select an ingredient. Next, have her feel its texture. After she smells the treat, invite her to taste it. Gimme five!

different types of cereal
semisweet mini chocolate chips
small crackers

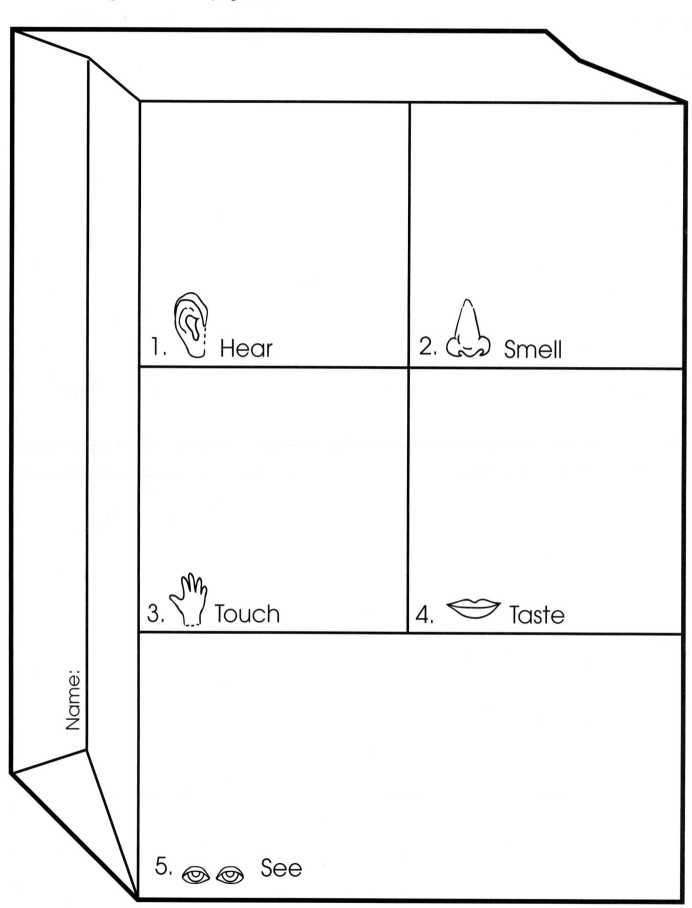

1. Hear

2. Smell

3. Touch

4. Taste

5. See

Name:

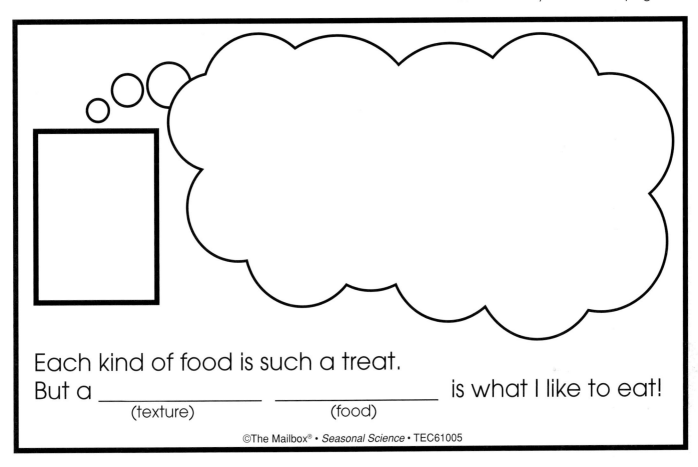

Each kind of food is such a treat.
But a _____ _____ is what I like to eat!
      (texture)   (food)

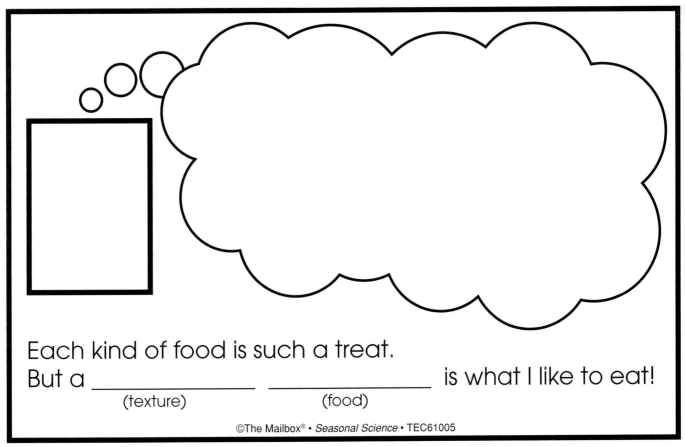

Each kind of food is such a treat.
But a _____ _____ is what I like to eat!
      (texture)   (food)

Soil Search

Invite your little ones to dig in and explore a very down-to-earth topic: soil!

An Earthy Mystery

Challenge your youngsters to unearth a scientific mystery with this inference activity. To prepare, cover a small oatmeal container and its lid with construction paper. Place two cups of garden soil in the container; then tightly secure the lid with tape. Begin the activity by seating your little scientists in a circle. Tell students that they are going to be learning about the mystery substance inside the container. Pass the container around the circle so that each child can feel its weight and listen as she shakes the container. Next, give students a few more clues about the container's contents by chanting the following riddle:

What is inside? What did I hide?
Its color is brown. To see it, look down.
It's crumbly and dry. It's not in the sky!
It's all around on the ground!

After each youngster has had a chance to guess the contents of the container, remove the lid and pass it around so that everyone can take a peek. Aha!

What do we know about soil?

It's brown. –Leah

If you put water in it, you can make mud. –Aaron

Plants grow in it. –Dustin

My dog likes to dig in it! –Kasey

Soil Exploration

Encourage your little ones to get down to the nitty-gritty of soil exploration with this hands-on investigation. To prepare, purchase a bag of garden soil at a garden center or discount store. Dump the soil into your sensory table and add some toy shovels and plastic cups. Then gather your group and ask them to tell you what they know about soil. Record their responses on a sheet of chart paper labeled as shown. Next, invite small groups to visit the sensory table to explore the appearance and texture of the soil. Encourage students' observations by asking questions. How does the soil smell? What does the soil feel like? What kind of things do you see in the soil? After everyone has had a chance to visit this down-and-dirty center, regroup and ask students to tell you more about soil; add the new observations to your chart. Then display the chart in your classroom. And keep a pen handy—your young scientists will have new discoveries to add!

A Soil Profile

Dig deeper in your soil search as you and your students make a model of the soil's layers. First, divide your class into three groups and give each group a large zippered plastic bag. Head outdoors and ask one group to hunt for rocks, another group to dig up some dirt, and the third group to gather decaying plant material, such as dead leaves or twigs. Return to your classroom and compare the weight, texture, and color of the materials in the three bags.

Next, bring out a large, clean, empty plastic jar. Explain that, together, you're going to build a model of what some soil looks like below the ground. Have student volunteers first put the rocks in the jar, then add a middle layer of dirt, and then put the plant matter on top. Explain that soil has a rocky underlayer, topped by a layer of dirt *(topsoil)*, and finished on the surface with a thin layer of decaying plant material *(humus)* that helps make the soil rich and healthy for plant growth. Place the lid on the jar and keep it on display for little ones to study. Then teach your students "Soil Layers Song" on this page to reinforce the demonstration.

Did You Know?

Humus is created when plant and animal materials decay. Humus enriches the topsoil with nutrients important to plants. It also improves the ability of the topsoil to absorb water.

Soil Layers Song

(sung to the tune of "Down by the Station")

Here is the soil that's all made up of layers.
There are special layers stacked up here to see.
See the rocks and stones here in the bottom layer?
Soil has layers—one, two, three!

Here is the soil that's all made up of layers.
There are special layers stacked up here to see.
See the topsoil that's in the middle layer?
Soil has layers—one, two, three!

Here is the soil that's all made up of layers.
There are special layers stacked up here to see.
See the humus here that's in the tip-top layer?
Soil has layers—one, two, three!

Did You Know?

If you were to cut straight down through the soil and remove the piece you've cut away, you'd see the layers that make up soil. The combination of different layers is called a *soil profile*. Each type of soil has a unique profile. Each layer in a soil profile is called a *horizon*.

Soil Profile Poster

Now that your little ones have helped make a model of the soil, they're ready to make these soil profile posters of their own. For each child, photocopy on white paper pages 126–128. Ask each child to cut out the layer labels on page 128; then guide him to glue each label to the corresponding box on his reproducibles. Next, have each child follow the instructions below to complete each poster panel. Once the child has decorated his panels, have him cut out each one along the heavy outline. Then help him glue his panels together as indicated.

Title Panel: Color the panel blue. Write your name on the line.
Panel 1: Draw a flower center just above the stem tip. Glue paper flower petals around the center. Color the background blue.
Panel 2: Color the stem and leaves green and the background blue. Glue bits of torn green, yellow, and brown paper to the panel on each side of the stem.
Panel 3: Color the roots tan. Color the background brown.
Panel 4: Color the background brown. Make black thumbprint "rocks" on the panel.

124

Soil Sorting

Ground your youngsters in the basics of classification with this soil-sorting activity. To prepare, gather several different kinds of soil, such as packaged garden soil, peat moss, potting soil, and plain sand. Divide each type of soil you've collected into three zippered freezer bags. Use clear packing tape to securely seal the top of each bag and prevent leaks. Then load all the bags into a child's wheelbarrow or wagon and wheel them into a center, along with a plastic flowerpot for each type of soil.

To use this center, a pair of youngsters studies the bags and groups together those that are alike, placing each group into a separate flowerpot. Once all your little ones have had a chance to try their hand at soil sorting, mix all the soils together and put some of the mix into each flowerpot. Add some flower seeds, a sprinkle of water, and the loving attention of your soil experts. You'll soon see your room in bloom!

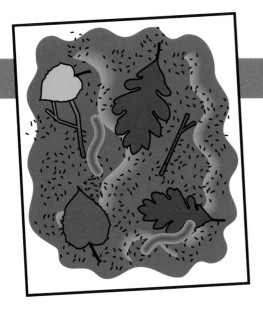

A Spectacular Soil Display

Wrap up your soil study with a delightful display of earthy items! First, have youngsters create fingerpaintings with brown paint. While the paint is still wet, sprinkle the contents of a dry tea bag over each child's painting. When the paint is dry, invite her to glue on a few twigs and leaves, and perhaps even a few pipe cleaner "worms"! Display the completed collages on a bulletin board. Position a table in front of the board and cover it with brown bulletin board paper. Display some books about soil, your flowerpots filled with soil (and maybe some sprouts!) from "Soil Sorting," and your soil profile jar (see "A Soil Profile" on page 123). Then hang your students' soil profile posters (page 124) all around the board to complete this educational exhibit about the science of soil!

Poster Panels

Use with "Soil Profile Poster" on page 124.

A Plant Grows
in Soil

by _____

Glue top of Panel 1 here.

1

Glue top of Panel 2 here.

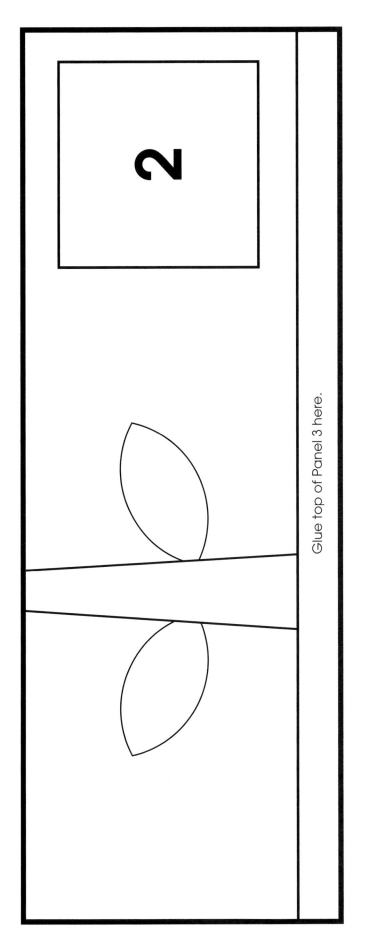

Glue top of Panel 3 here.

Glue top of Panel 4 here.

Poster Panel and Labels
Use with "Soil Profile Poster" on page 124.

©The Mailbox® • *Seasonal Science* • TEC61005

1

The Plant

2

The Top Layer

leaves
twigs
bugs

3

The Middle Layer

soil

4

The Bottom Layer

rocks

Spring Selections

Help your little ones greet the coming of spring with these seasonal stories.

When Spring Comes

Written and Photo-Illustrated by Robert Maass

Springtime is the right time for your budding scientists to observe the world around them. *When Spring Comes* blooms with colorful photos and descriptions of springtime sights. Read the book aloud, allowing time for students to comment on the spring objects and activities in the story. After you've read and discussed the book, encourage your youngsters to dictate a list of other sights they might see in the spring. Then help students classify the sights under separate headings such as the ones shown. Later, invite each child to fill a minibooklet with her favorite signs of spring. Duplicate the booklet cover and pages (page 131) on white paper for each child. Have the child cut out her booklet cover and pages, sequence them, and then staple the resulting booklet in the upper-left corner. Encourage each child to personalize her booklet by illustrating each page with one of her favorite things to complement the text. Conclude the activity by inviting each child to read her booklet aloud so that she can share her favorite springtime observations with classmates.

In the Rain With Baby Duck

Written by Amy Hest
Illustrated by Jill Barton

Baby Duck's reaction to a rainstorm almost ruins her day, but Grampa Duck remembers that sometimes it takes special rain gear to make wet weather feel wonderful! After sharing this tale with your youngsters, invite them to discuss what rain gear helps them stay nice and dry in a spring shower. Encourage each child to predict which color of raincoat is the most popular in the class. Then follow up with this graphing activity. Give each child a copy of the survey recording sheet (page 132) and help him complete the top portion. Next, ask him to color the large raincoat at the bottom of the page to look like his own; then have him cut it out and post it on a prepared graph. Invite students to discuss the completed graph and decide which color of raincoat is the most popular. Then have each child return to his survey sheet and record the most popular raincoat color. Your little ones will eagerly look forward to showing off their colorful gear on the next rainy day!

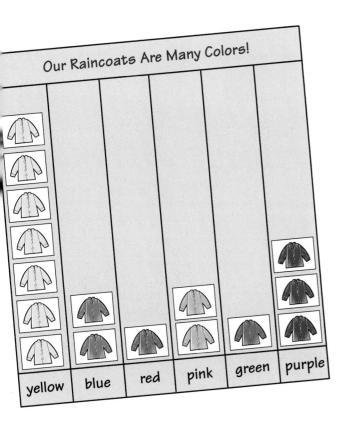

One Bean

Written by Anne Rockwell
Illustrated by Megan Halsey

Sprout some fun when you share *One Bean,* a step-by-step story that centers around a simple little legume. As you read the book, discuss the similarities of the bean sprout with the sprouts studied in the unit on pages 111–116. After reading, return to the page that describes what the boy sees when he investigates the inside of a ripe green bean. Next, show students a bowl of fresh, raw green beans, and ask them if they think they will find the same kinds of little seeds inside. Then invite your group to take a peek inside three beans with this engaging activity!

Give each child a copy of the lab report on page 133. Use a toothpick to split open a beanpod and count the seeds. Instruct each child to draw a matching number of seeds inside bean A on her lab report. Repeat the process for each remaining bean. Help her use the data to draw conclusions and then complete her report.

A Nest Full of Eggs

Written by Priscilla Belz Jenkins
Illustrated by Lizzy Rockwell

There's nothing like watching the robins build their safe, cozy nests from common materials each spring. After you've read aloud *A Nest Full of Eggs,* review the nest-building pictures. Have students list items that the robins use to build their nest. Then stock a nest-making center with those materials as well as shredded newspaper, yarn, string, crinkled paper strips, and Easter grass. Provide each child in this center with a personalized, individual-size pie tin, a paintbrush, and a squeeze bottle of brown-tinted glue.

To make one robin's nest craft, squeeze an amount of glue into the pie tin and spread it around with the paintbrush to coat the interior. Press into the glue a slightly overlapping layer of nest materials; then set it aside to dry. Glue a second layer of materials to the nest, building it into a cup shape as described in the book. When the nest is dry, gently press the sides of the child's pan to loosen the nest and remove it. To complete the activity, duplicate the nest materials recording sheet (page 134) on brown paper to make a class supply. Ask each little builder to glue a sample of her preferred nest materials to the sheet. Arrange each child's nest model along with her recording sheet on a table to create a constructive display!

2

Here's an outside game I like to play.

5

My favorite sign of spring is _____.

1

It's a baby animal's birthday.

4

...brings a Maytime flower.

Signs
of
Spring

by _____

©The Mailbox® • *Seasonal Science* • TEC61005

3

A soft April shower...

My Rain Gear Survey

 **Circle** the items that you use.

 hat   boots   umbrella   raincoat

What color is **your** raincoat?

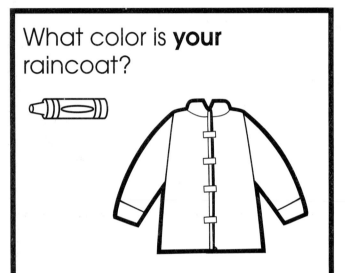

What do you think is the **most popular** color?

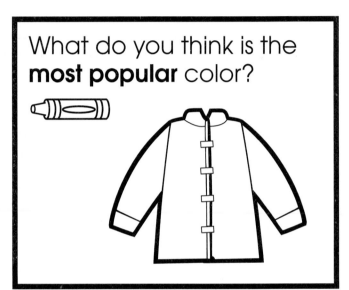

The most popular raincoat color in our class is…

 Write.

_____

_ _ _ _ _ _ _ _ _ _ _ _ _ _ _

_____

A Three-Bean Study

✏️ Draw the seeds.   ✏️ Write the number.

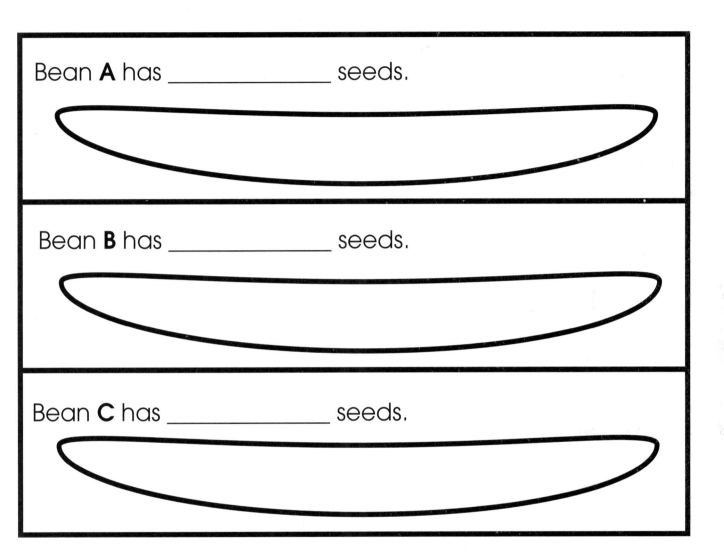

Bean **A** has _____ seeds.

Bean **B** has _____ seeds.

Bean **C** has _____ seeds.

✏️ Write **A, B,** or **C.**

This bean has the **most** seeds. _____

This bean has the **fewest** seeds. _____

Do any beans have the **same** number of seeds? _____

Note to the teacher: Use with *One Bean* on page 130.

Nest Materials Recording Sheet

Use with *A Nest Full of Eggs* on page 130.

Here Is the Nest
That _____
name
Built!

My nest is made of **mud** and...

Investigating Crayons

Red, yellow, green, purple, orange, and blue—this colorful unit is ready for you!

What's in the Bag?

Color your young scientists curious when you begin your crayon studies with this inference activity. In advance, place a crayon in a paper lunch bag. Rattle the bag to attract youngsters' attention; then sing the song below. Dramatically read each of the clues to your young-sters; after revealing each one, encourage them to guess the bag's contents.

(sung to the tune of "The Wheels on the Bus")

What's in the bag? Oh, can you guess?
Can you guess? Can you guess?
What's in the bag? Oh, can you guess?
Here are some clues.

Clues:
1. It's small enough to be in this bag.
2. When I use it, it gets smaller and smaller.
3. It is usually wrapped in paper.
4. Sometimes it breaks.
5. It comes in different colors.
6. You can draw, write, and color with it.

   Invite youngsters to take one last guess; then reveal the bag's contents. It's a crayon, of course! Reread the clues to confirm that they do indeed describe a crayon.

And the Winner Is...

Crayons come in many beautiful hues, but everyone has a special favorite! Predicting and comparing are just a couple of the skills involved in this colorful graphing idea. In advance, prepare a large graph by labeling it with the eight common crayon colors (red, blue, yellow, green, orange, purple, brown, black). Provide each child with a copy of a crayon pattern from page 138. Next, ask each child to predict which color will be the class favorite as you record responses on a chart. Then have each child personalize his pattern, color it with his favorite crayon shade, and then cut it out. Invite each student to attach his pattern to the appropriate column on the graph; then discuss the results. So what's your students' favorite color of crayon?

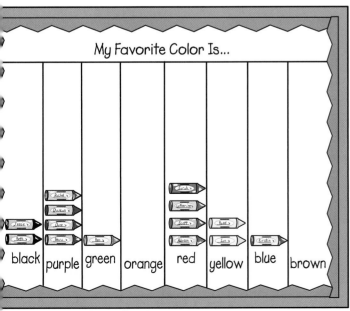

Shining Through

Here's a nifty small-group experiment that your little scientists won't be able to resist! In advance, gather a class supply of 12" x 18" construction paper and brightly colored crayons (fluorescent ones work well). Mix up a batch of blue tempera paint thinned with water. You'll also need paintbrushes and a supply of paper towels.

Invite each youngster to fold a sheet of paper in half and then use crayons to lightly draw on one half of her paper. Next, direct her to bear down heavily as she draws more crayon pictures on the other half of the page. Invite each child to brush a thin wash of paint across her entire page and then wipe off any excess with a paper towel. Encourage youngsters to discuss the differences and similarities they see between the two halves of their paintings. Ask youngsters if they think the paint consistency affected the results. Then extend the experiment by inviting students to try various thicknesses of paint on more crayon resists.

This Is Why

Crayons are made from pigments and liquid paraffin wax; wax resists water. The water-based tempera paint soaked into the construction paper, but not where the crayon was heavily colored. The paint was unable to penetrate the paper because the wax in the crayon resisted the paint.

Earth Day Meltdown

Here's a grand way to celebrate Earth Day, or any day! To prepare, personalize a five-ounce paper cup for each child. Gather muffin tins, crayon shavings, and old peeled crayon pieces. Invite each child in a small group to place approximately one inch of crayon pieces and shavings into his cup and then place it into a muffin tin compartment. Place the tin in a 350-degree oven for approximately five minutes, or until the crayon pieces have just melted. Remove the tins from the oven and allow the crayon cups to cool completely. Then direct each child to peel the paper cup from his "new" crayon. If desired, conclude the activity by having students use their new crayons to draw step-by-step picture cards depicting how they made them. For an *extra* special Earth Day, why not make "earth" crayons by melting only blue and green crayon pieces and shavings?

This Is Why

Crayons have a low melting point, which refers to the temperature at which a solid turns to liquid. When the melted crayons cool, they harden into solids again.

My Crayon

You can shave it, melt it, make rubbings with it…there are plenty of things to do with a crayon! Making this discovery booklet will be heaps of fun for little hands.

Materials for each booklet:
white construction paper copy of the booklet cover and pages (pages 139–142)
scissors
crayons
plastic needlepoint mesh or burlap
handheld pencil sharpener
glue
two 8" x 2½" sheets of waxed paper
iron set on the lowest temperature (and an adult volunteer)
thin tempera paint (any color)
paintbrushes

To make one booklet:
Read the booklet aloud. Cut out the booklet cover and pages; then follow these suggestions to complete each page.

Cover: Color the crayon with your favorite color. Write your name on the line.

Page 1: Trace the line with your crayon.

Page 2: Color the page with the side of your crayon.

Page 3: Make a rubbing with your crayon.

Page 4: Using a handheld pencil sharpener, make a few crayon shavings. Glue them to the page.

Page 5: Make more crayon shavings. Sandwich them between two sheets of waxed paper; then have an adult iron them together. After the waxed paper has cooled, trim it and glue it to the page.

Page 6: Draw a picture using heavy strokes. Paint over your drawing with contrasting paint.

Page 7: Draw a picture of an object that is the same color as your crayon.

My Crayon
by Gwen

I can trace with my crayon. 1
I can color with the side of my crayon. 2
I can make a rubbing with my crayon. 3
I can shave my crayon. 4
I can melt my crayon. 5
I can paint over my crayon. 6
apple redbird
I can draw a picture with my crayon. 7

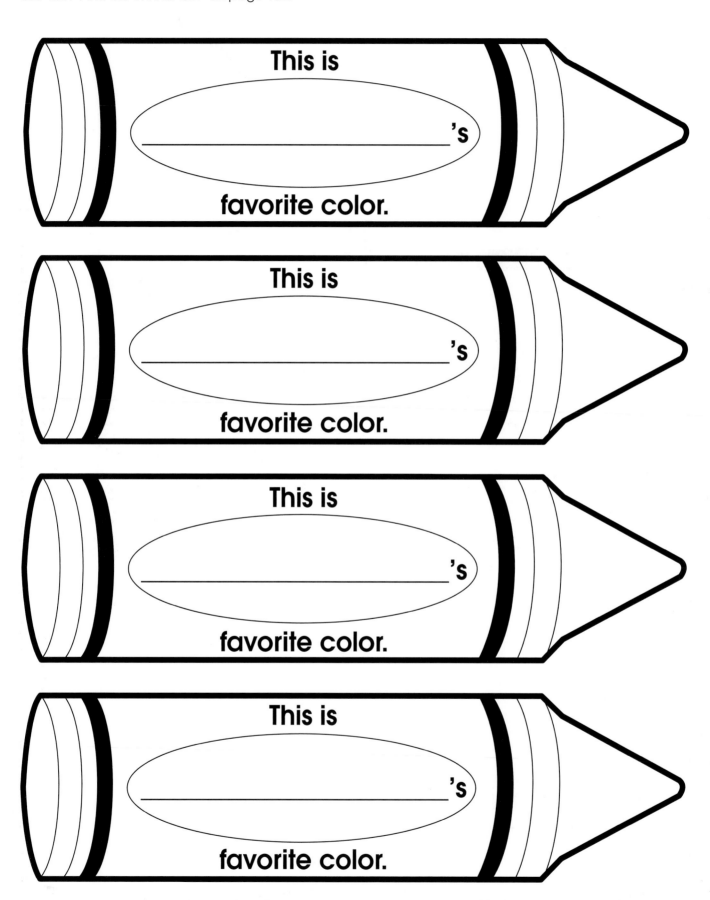

This is
_____'s
favorite color.

This is
_____'s
favorite color.

This is
_____'s
favorite color.

This is
_____'s
favorite color.

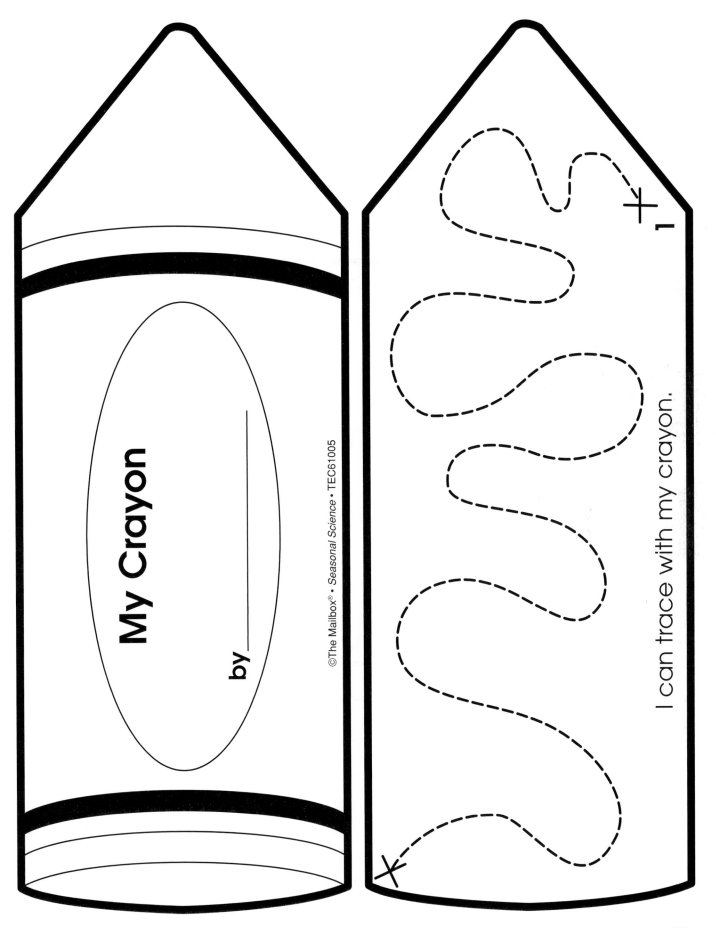

My Crayon

by _____

©The Mailbox® • Seasonal Science • TEC61005

I can trace with my crayon.

1

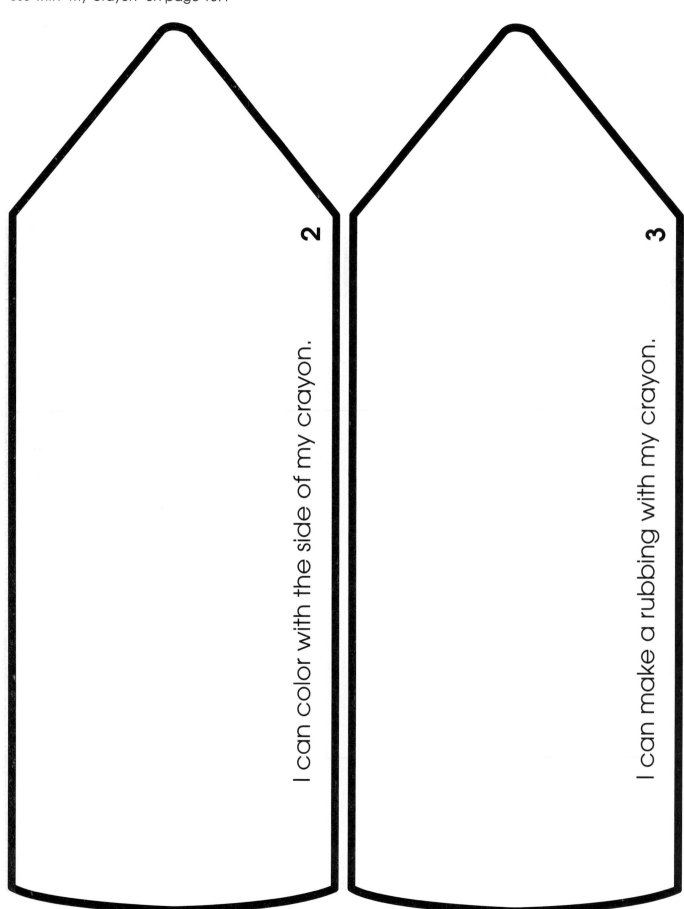

2

I can color with the side of my crayon.

3

I can make a rubbing with my crayon.

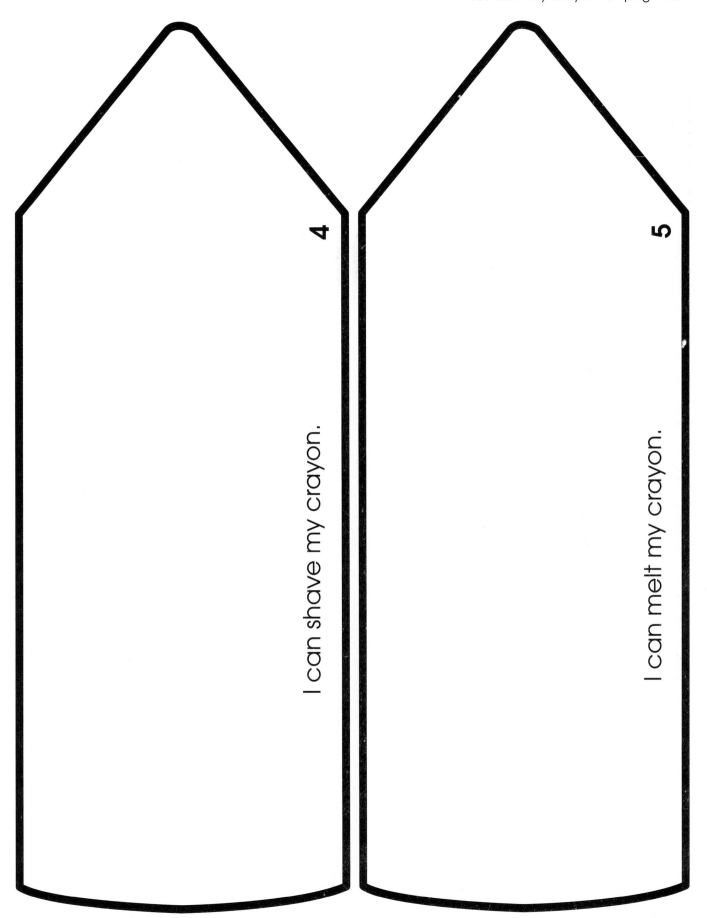

4

I can shave my crayon.

5

I can melt my crayon.

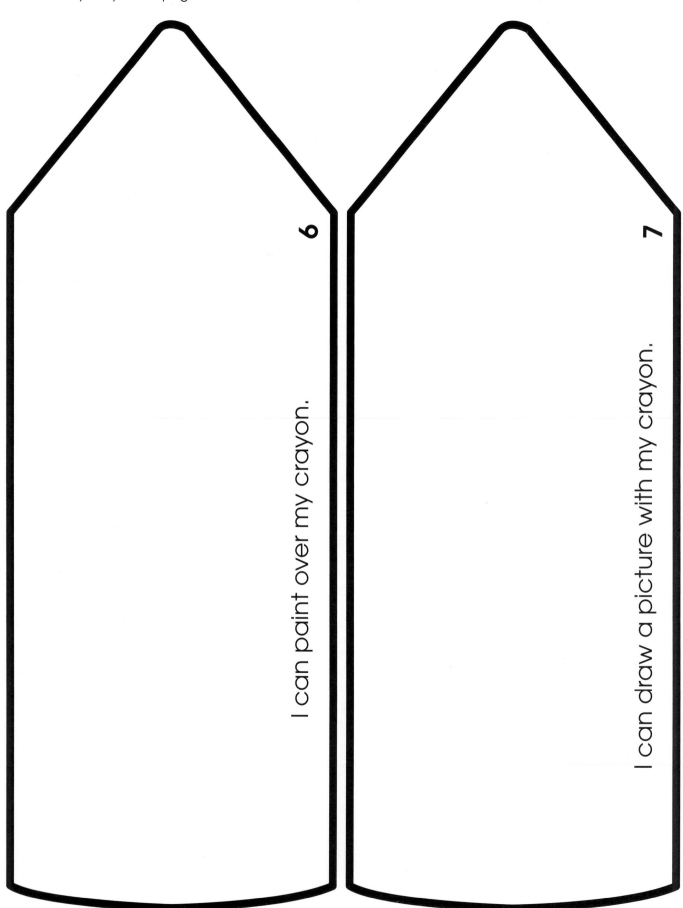

6

I can paint over my crayon.

7

I can draw a picture with my crayon.

Healthful Habits Head to Toe

Get every body in tip-top shape with this introduction to good health habits.

Good for Me

Here's a musical introduction to the topic of good health habits. Before teaching the following song to your students, ask them to identify some healthful habits. Guide them to include such things as exercising, getting a good night's sleep, staying clean, and eating nutritious foods. Jot their suggestions on a sheet of chart paper labeled "What's Good for Me?" Then teach little ones this song, substituting phrases from the chart for the underlined words each time you repeat the verse.

(sung to the tune of "The Wheels on the Bus")

[Healthful habits] are good for me,
Good for me, good for me.
[Healthful habits] are good for me
All day long!

What's Good for Me?

eating vegetables—Trisha
drinking milk—Piel
going to bed on time—Janae
taking a nap—Robert
playing outside—Ellie

Listen to music.

Take a bath.

Read a book.

Sleep Secrets

Big or little, young or old—everyone does it. What is it? Sleep! Share the following facts about sleep with your little ones. Then ask your students to share some ways they settle down before going to sleep. How about taking a bath? Reading a book? Or listening to music? Record each suggestion on a pastel-colored construction paper pillow shape. Display the pillow cutouts on a classroom wall. You may want to review these settling-down techniques (at least the ones that are classroom-appropriate) when rest time rolls around!

Sleep Facts
- Sleep is a natural process that allows a person's body to rest and repair itself.
- Children need more sleep than adults.
- Most children between the ages of three and six sleep from 10 to 12 hours each day.
- Our brains need sleep! Without sleep, people can become irritable and forget things easily.

Wash Your Hands

This small-group activity is a handy way to demonstrate the basics of germ removal! In advance, gather an eyedropper for each child in a small group. You'll also need a pie pan filled with vegetable oil, two buckets of warm water, some liquid soap, and paper towels.

Invite each child in the group to fill his eyedropper with oil. Have him squirt the oil into the palm of one hand and then rub the oil over both hands. Explain that the oil is like germs. You get germs on your hands from many things that you touch throughout the day. How can your little ones get rid of these oil "germs"? By washing their hands! Bring out one of the buckets of warm water and ask each child to wash his hands *without* soap. Ask your youngsters if the oil "germs" are gone from their hands. Explain that germs can be washed away only if soap is used. Then bring out the second bucket of water and give each of your young scientists a squirt of liquid soap. Encourage youngsters to lather up and scrub for about 15 seconds.

Don't Share Your Sneezes!

Ahhh-choo! Are students sneezing in your classroom? Seize this teachable moment and demonstrate to youngsters why sneezes shouldn't be shared. Bring a spray bottle of water to your group time. Spray some water on a sheet of colored construction paper as your group watches. Explain that when we sneeze, germs travel out of our mouths and noses and into the air for others to breathe. So if you share a sneeze, you're also sharing germs! Next, cover the spray bottle nozzle with a tissue and make the bottle "sneeze" into the tissue. Did the tissue stop the sneeze? You bet! Then give each child a chance to make the bottle "sneeze" into a fresh tissue. Wrap up this activity with a catchy tune to help youngsters remember how to put the freeze on the germs from a sneeze!

(sung to the tune of "Pop! Goes the Weasel")

When you feel a sneeze coming on,
You sure don't want to share it!
Grab a tissue as quick as you can.
DON'T share your sneezes!

Smart Snacks

Teach your little ones to keep those good health habits going all day by choosing good-for-you snacks. First, ask students to brainstorm a list of snack foods as you write their ideas on a sheet of chart paper. Explain that eating a snack is a great way to get more energy and nutrients into your body. But it should be a smart snack! A smart snack helps your body get energy and nutrients, tastes good, and is low in fat, sugar, and salt. So what's the perfect smart snack? Fruit! Ask youngsters to brainstorm a list of fruits as you write their responses on another sheet of chart paper. Then ask each child to choose her favorite fruit from the list and illustrate it on a 12" x 18" sheet of white construction paper. Add a line of text to each child's drawing. Then stack all the pages between poster board covers and bind the book along the left side. Title this mouthwatering book "Smart Snacks" and decorate the cover with fruit stickers, perhaps scented ones. Add this yummy book to your class library.

AJ likes oranges for a snack.

Fresh and Fruity Snacks

Eating fruit is one healthful habit you don't want little ones to forget! So have students illustrate these booklets and take them home as reminders of this smart—and scrumptious—snack! Duplicate the booklet cover and text strips on page 147 for each child. Cut five 5" x 8" blank booklet pages per child. Read through the directions below and gather the necessary materials.

Working with one small group at a time, help students read through the text strips and then cut them apart. Direct each child to glue one strip to each of her blank booklet pages. Then have each child illustrate her pages according to the suggestions below. Later, help each student sequence the pages and then staple the booklet along the left side.

Cover: Write your name on the line. Draw and color different fruits.
Page 1: Make green tempera paint thumbprints.
Page 2: Glue on orange construction paper triangles.
Page 3: Cut heart shapes from red tissue paper. Glue them to the page; then use a correction pen or a toothpick dipped in yellow tempera paint to add "seeds."
Page 4: Sponge-paint watermelon chunks. When the paint is dry, use a thin black marker to add "seeds."
Page 5: Use markers to draw your favorite fruit; then write its name on the line.

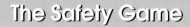

The Safety Game

Being healthy means being safe, so use this variation on a classic game to review some good safety practices. Explain to your students that you are going to read a series of statements (see below) and that they must decide as a group whether each statement is safe or unsafe. If the group decides correctly, they will get one letter in the word *safety* written on the chalkboard. Once they've spelled the entire word, they'll get a reward, such as an extra ten minutes of *safe* play on the playground!

If desired, make this a team game. Divide your class into two teams and have the teams compete to see who can spell the word *safety* first. Add additional safety statements the next time you play to keep the game fresh.

Safe!

- Always look both ways before crossing the street.
- It is okay to play in the street.
- Cross the street at a crosswalk.
- It is okay to play with matches.
- Cross the street without looking both ways.
- Remember your phone number and address.
- Don't talk to strangers.
- It's okay to ride a bike without a helmet.
- Keep your fingers away from electrical outlets.
- Always swim alone.
- You don't need to know your address.
- Stay with your family in a crowded place.
- Always buckle up in the car.

Hip, Hip, Hooray for Helmets!

When it comes to healthful habits, wearing a helmet for sports activities is at the top of the list! Encourage all your students (and their parents) to wear helmets for biking and skating by holding a Helmet Day at school. Send home a note asking that students who have them bring their helmets to school. Bring in your own bicycle helmet and demonstrate the proper way to wear it. Inform students that the helmet should sit squarely on top of the head and cover the forehead. Help each child who has brought in her helmet put it on properly. Then invite your helmeted youngsters to sing the following song to stress the importance of wearing helmets. Complete your Helmet Day activities by inviting youngsters to enjoy an extended playtime with your ride-on toys—wearing their helmets, of course!

(sung to the tune of "If You're Happy and You Know It")

Wear a helmet when you [bike] — put it on!
Wear a helmet when you [bike] — put it on!
If you have a little wreck,
Then your head it will protect!
Wear a helmet when you [bike] — put it on!

Repeat the verse, substituting the word skate *for the underlined word.*

I LIKE FRUIT!

by _____

I like to eat grapes.	**1**
I like to eat cantaloupe.	**2**
I like to eat strawberries.	**3**
I like to eat watermelon.	**4**
I like to eat _____.	**5**

Getting in Touch With Texture

Bumpy, furry, smooth—this texture unit is full of real feel appeal!

That Certain Feeling

Touch base with textures as your youngsters feel their way through this hands-on investigation. In advance, fill a large feely bag or a pillowcase with a variety of textured items (see the list below for ideas). Label a set of cards with different texture words such as *soft, rough,* and *smooth.* Place the cards and bag in the center of your circle area.

Begin the activity by explaining to your group that each object in the bag has a particular type of feel, or *texture,* that our fingers recognize. Next, challenge your group to test their tactile abilities. Sing the song at right, naming both a child and texture where indicated. Invite that child to reach into the bag for the object. Then ask her to pair the object with its corresponding word card. Repeat the song several times with different students and textures. For more practice and fun, place the feely bag, texture items, and word cards in a center for pairs of students to further explore!

Soft	Rough	Smooth
cotton balls	sandpaper	flat plastic lid
yarn	pinecone	plastic egg
towel	scrub pad	rubber eraser
stuffed animal	Styrofoam ball	hard rubber ball

(sung to the tune of "Mary Had a Little Lamb")

Can [child's name] find something [soft],
Something [soft], something [soft]?
Can [child's name] find something [soft]
In our feely bag?
[Child's name] found something [soft],
Something [soft], something [soft].
[Child's name] found something [soft]
In our feely bag.

Alex touched something soft. It was yarn.

Picture That Feeling

Continue the feely fun with this picture-perfect display. In advance, program a sheet of paper with the sentences "_____ touched something _____. It was _____." Then copy it to make a class supply. Explain to youngsters that every object has a *texture* that they feel because of special touch receptors inside their fingers. Give each child a copy of the programmed sheet and ask him to write his name on the first blank line. Invite each child to draw a picture of something he discovered in the feely bag. Then help him complete the sentences as shown. Mount the finished texture pictures on a bulletin board titled "Picture That Feeling." Also mount small samples of the pictured texture objects for a truly textural display!

Texture Treasures

Track down textures with this treasure hunt activity. To prepare, label a set of cards with texture words (or use the cards from "That Certain Feeling" on page 148) and then collect several lunch-size paper bags. Divide your youngsters into small groups and then give each group a texture word card and a bag. Instruct each group to fill its bag with items that match its assigned texture. Later, invite each group to share the items it has collected; then challenge classmates to guess the group's texture word. Now that's textural treasure!

Did You Know?

Our skin helps us collect information. When we touch something, our skin detects whether it is rough, smooth, or bumpy. Skin contains *nerve endings* that send messages about touch to our brains.

The Eyes Have It

Focus your youngsters' attention on sight as a way to describe textures with this sensory activity. Share the wordless book *Is It Rough? Is It Smooth? Is It Shiny?* by Tana Hoban with your children. Encourage youngsters to carefully observe the photographs on each page; then discuss how each pictured object may *feel* to the touch. Explain to students that shiny objects are slick, or smooth-textured enough to reflect light. Next, ask youngsters to describe the textures. Record their responses on a chart as shown. Extend this activity by showing youngsters a variety of textured objects and having them guess how each one might feel. Then invite youngsters to touch each object to determine whether their hypothesis was correct. What a smooth idea!

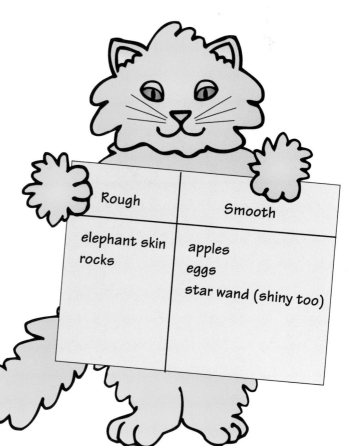

Rough	Smooth
elephant skin	apples
rocks	eggs
	star wand (shiny too)

Art With Feeling

Put some real feeling into your youngsters' paintings with this tactile activity. To prepare, gather art paper and several different colors of both washable tempera paint and finger-paint. Add texture to some of the paint by mixing in various amounts of glitter, sand, or soap flakes. Also collect various paint tools, such as sponges, toothbrushes, aluminum foil balls, plastic wrap balls, and cotton balls.

Invite a small group of students to your art table. Encourage each child to experiment with the different paints, tools, and, of course, their fingers! As the children are painting, discuss the many textures in the paint and the effects made by their fingers and the tools. Bet they'll have lots to say about this touchy-feely art!

Touchable Portraits

Youngsters will enjoy putting the finishing touches on self-portraits with this imaginative art idea. To prepare, collect one sturdy paper plate for each child, a hand mirror, white glue, a construction paper conversation balloon, and various textured art supplies (see the list below for suggestions). Ask each child in a small group to observe himself in the mirror. Then give him a paper plate and guide him as he uses the textural supplies to create a stunning self-portrait. When the portraits are dry, display each one with a personalized conversation balloon as shown. Darling, you look fabulous!

Textured art supplies:

faux fur	felt	wiggle eyes
pipe cleaners	feathers	stickers
fabric	craft foam	pom-poms
sandpaper	cotton balls	crepe paper
yarn	tissue	crinkle strips
foil	waxed paper	bubble wrap

150

Ready, Set, Rub!

Buff up fine-motor skills with this texture-rubbing activity. In advance, create texture templates by drawing a different shape on each of several poster board squares with a thick line of glue (for colorful templates, tint the glue with tempera paint) as shown. Let the templates dry overnight; then securely tape each one to a tabletop (or similar surface) in your art center. Model the process of texture rubbing for your youngsters. Give a small group of children several sheets of white paper, crayons, colored pencils, and markers; then encourage them to experiment and create different rubbings. Extend the activity by inviting each child to mount her favorite rubbing on a folded sheet of construction paper to make a personalized card for a loved one.

Texture Rubbings

Are your little ones ready to try some independent rubbings? Then have them make these booklets. In advance, copy the booklet cover on page 152 for each child. Next, assemble a rubbings tool kit for each child by placing several 4½" x 7" sheets of copy paper, a peeled crayon, and a sharp pencil into a resealable plastic bag. Divide youngsters into small groups and give each child her tool kit. Instruct each group to search for textured surfaces to make a different rubbing on each sheet, such as floor tile, a brick wall, a sidewalk, and a leaf. Assist each youngster in writing the object name on each rubbing sheet. Later, give each child a booklet cover to personalize and color. Then help each child stack all her pages behind the cover and staple them together along the left side. Encourage youngsters to take their texture booklets home to read to their families. What a neat way to keep in touch!

Tactile Match

Feel the excitement as your little matchmakers play this center game. To prepare, use paper and crayons to create rubbings of several common classroom and household items, such as a comb, puzzle pieces, a ruler, and safety scissors. Then place the real objects and the rubbing sheets at the center. Invite a small group of youngsters to match each real object with its rubbed representation. How perceptive!

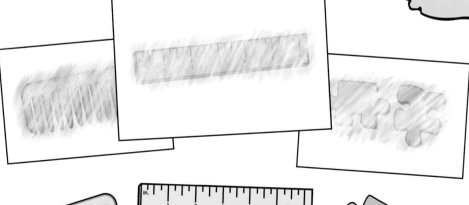

My
Texture Rubbings
Booklet

by

_____

©The Mailbox® • *Seasonal Science* • TEC61005

My
Texture Rubbings
Booklet

by

_____

©The Mailbox® • *Seasonal Science* • TEC61005

The Word on Birds

The word is out—birds are some of the most interesting critters around! No matter where you live, your fledgling bird-watchers should be able to spy some of our most common feathered friends. So come on and wing into spring!

Recognizing Robins

Introduce your bird study by inviting students to make the acquaintance of a fine-feathered mystery guest! Duplicate the robin patterns on page 155 on white construction paper. Color the wing, tail, head, and back of the robin's body brown. Color the breast red, the beak yellow, and the legs gray. Leave the throat white. Then cut out all the pieces and prepare them for use on your flannelboard. (Be sure to glue felt to the robin's body where you want to attach the wing and tail.)

At a group time, recite the rhyme below, pausing at the end of each line for students' guesses. Once students have guessed that the mystery visitor is a bird, put the robin together on your flannelboard. Ask youngsters to name the bird's body parts as you go. Then introduce your new bird friend as a robin. Tell your students that many people consider the appearance of robins on their lawn as a sure sign that spring has arrived!

A mystery guest is here today. It is a living thing.
It has two legs. It has two eyes. It really likes to sing!
It has a tail. It has a beak. It flaps two wings to fly.
Sometimes it hops across the grass. Sometimes it's in the sky.

Hopping Robin Puppets

Now that your little ones know what a robin looks like, encourage them to put together their own robin puppets. Duplicate the robin patterns on page 155 on white construction paper to make a class supply. Have each child use your flannelboard robin as a guide for coloring the parts of her puppet. Then help her cut out the pieces and attach the wing, tail, and beak to the robin's body with brads. Have her glue the puppet to a wide craft stick. Then get those robins hoppin' to the following tune!

(sung to the tune of "Bingo")

The robin hops across the lawn. It's looking for a worm, oh!
R-O-B-I-N, R-O-B-I-N, R-O-B-I-N,
The robin [flicks his tail], oh!   *Move the puppet's tail up and down.*

Repeat the verse two more times, substituting the following phrases and motions:
flaps its wing   *Move the puppet's wing up and down.*
moves its beak   *Open and close the puppet's beak.*

We're Going on a Worm Hunt

Why does a robin spend the morning hopping across the grass? It's catching wiggly worms for breakfast! Invite your youngsters to imitate robins when they go on a worm hunt of their own. To prepare for this activity, which will challenge your students' observation skills, cut ten two-inch pieces each of brown, white, and green yarn. Scatter the yarn pieces on a grassy area outdoors. Then ask students to imagine they are hungry, sharp-eyed robins. Tell them they'll be hunting for brown, white, and green yarn "worms" outside. Then take them to the prepared hunting ground and set them loose as you sing this song to the tune of "London Bridge."

> Hungry robins look for worms, look for worms, look for worms.
> Hungry robins look for worms in the green grass.
>
> Hungry robins find some worms, find some worms, find some worms.
> Hungry robins find some worms in the green grass.

After you've sung both verses of the song, have students stop their search and head indoors, even if they've left some worms behind. Then continue with the graphing activity described below.

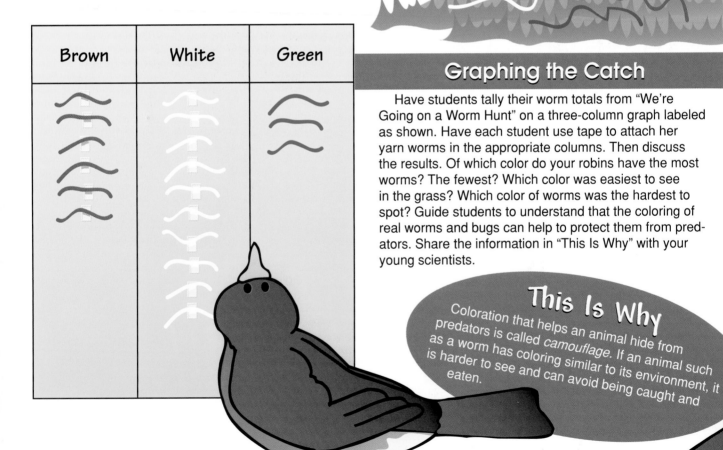

Brown	White	Green

Graphing the Catch

Have students tally their worm totals from "We're Going on a Worm Hunt" on a three-column graph labeled as shown. Have each student use tape to attach her yarn worms in the appropriate columns. Then discuss the results. Of which color do your robins have the most worms? The fewest? Which color was easiest to see in the grass? Which color of worms was the hardest to spot? Guide students to understand that the coloring of real worms and bugs can help to protect them from predators. Share the information in "This Is Why" with your young scientists.

This Is Why

Coloration that helps an animal hide from predators is called *camouflage*. If an animal such as a worm has coloring similar to its environment, it is harder to see and can avoid being caught and eaten.

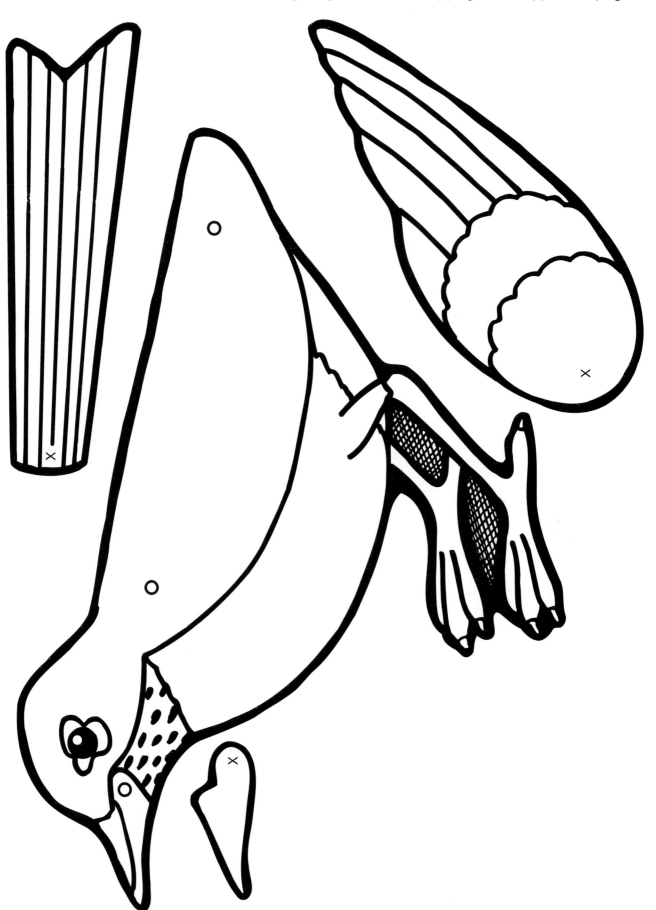

Bubbles, Bubbles Everywhere!

These discovery ideas will have your youngsters bursting with excitement for bubbleology—the science of bubbles!

Whisked Away by Bubbles

Introduce your little ones to sudsy bubbles with this small-group activity. In advance, have a parent donate a bottle of clear dishwashing liquid. Half-fill your sensory table with water; then place several wire whisks (or rotary eggbeaters) nearby. Ask your students to predict whether bubbles can be made with plain water; then invite them to use the whisks to find out. Students will conclude that something else is needed to produce bubbles. Next, tell students that you have a magic bubble solution. Dramatically squirt some dishwashing liquid into the water. Then ask each child to predict what will happen when they use the whisks in the water this time. With just a flick of the wrist, your youngsters will see bunches and bunches of bubbles!

This Is Why

A bubble is air that is trapped inside a liquid. Water does not produce bubbles because its molecules cling to each other, causing *surface tension*. Adding soap to the water weakens the surface tension and makes the water stretchy enough to form a bubble.

Billions of Bright Bubbles!

Involve your little ones in making different-colored bubble mixtures for future outdoor use! Follow the recipe below to help your students make several batches. For best results, let the mixtures sit for at least five days before using. Before the bubble-blowing event, ask your students to predict whether the added food coloring will affect the color of the bubbles. Then invite your little learners to blow as many bubbles as they can. Oooh—bright bubbles!

Bright Bubbles
5 tbsp. soft water (or use distilled water)
4 tbsp. clear Dawn dishwashing liquid
1 tbsp. light corn syrup
5 drops food coloring

Stir Up Some Syrup Solution!

Pop! Bubbles don't tend to stay around very long. Involve your little scientists in discovering longer-lasting bubbles with this fun activity. In advance, make two batches of bubble solution by mixing five tablespoons of water with four tablespoons of Dawn dish detergent in separate plastic containers. Add one tablespoon of light corn syrup to one of the mixtures; then label the container. Gather several bubble wands or make pipe cleaner wands similar to the one shown. Ask a group of students to brainstorm reasons bubbles burst so quickly. Then invite each child to blow a bubble from the first mixture and count how many seconds until the bubble pops. Have him repeat the activity with the corn syrup mixture. After comparing, your little ones will conclude that syrup is the solution to stronger bubbles!

This Is Why

Bubbles pop because the soapy solution dries, releasing the air inside them. Adding corn syrup (or glycerine) helps the bubbles hold more water, which makes them stronger.

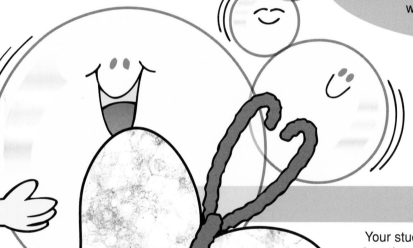

"Bubble-fly" Art

Your students will be bubbling over with enthusiasm when they make these lasting impressions of bubbles! In advance, enlarge and make two copies of the butterfly pattern on page 160 for each child. Gather a class supply of drinking straws and pipe cleaners. Then use the recipe below to make several colored bubble solutions, each in a separate yogurt cup. To paint one butterfly, use a straw to blow into the bubble solution.

When bubbles have risen slightly above the rim, gently press a section of the butterfly on the bubbles. Repeat using different colors; then set the butterfly aside to dry. Next, bend a pipe cleaner in half and secure it to the butterfly by twisting the pipe cleaner as shown. Curl the ends to resemble antennae. Display these beautiful "bubble-flies" for all to enjoy!

Bubble Paint Solution
½ c. water
¼ c. Dawn dishwashing liquid
2 tsp. tempera paint

A Book of Bubbles

Engage students in this booklet-making project and they will bubble over with excitement! To prepare, duplicate page 159 and the bottom portion of 160 to make a class supply. Gather the necessary supplies; then help each student follow the suggestions below to complete her pages. To bind each booklet, sequence the pages behind the cover and staple along the left-hand side. Send the completed booklets home for some good clean reading fun!

Cover: Print your name on the line. Color the bubble.
Page 1: Color the ruler. Make several bubble prints using paint and a juice can.
Page 2: Color the ruler. Make several bubble prints using paint and a film canister.
Page 3: Print the numeral 3 in the box. Make three bubble prints using paint and a small round sponge.
Page 4: Use the bubble paint solution from "'Bubble-fly' Art" on page 157 to blow colorful bubbles onto a half-sheet of white paper. When the paint is dry, cut out a small circle. Glue your colorful bubble to the page.

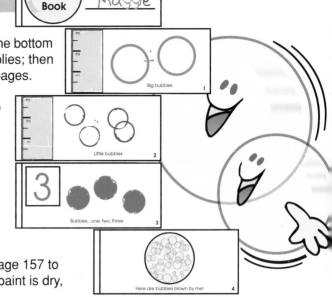

Shake It Up!

Shake, shake, shake.
One, two, three.
How many bubbles
Will we see?

Use this simple experiment to show your little ones that some soaps make better bubbles! To prepare, have parents donate a bottle of baby shampoo and a bottle of dish detergent. Label two resealable plastic bags as shown. Gather your students and have each child predict which soap will produce more bubbles. Then add one cup of water and one-fourth teaspoon of each kind of soap into its labeled bag. Recite the rhyme above while each student takes a turn shaking the bags. After a few rounds of the rhyme, have students determine which soap worked best for making lots of tiny bubbles. Shake it up, baby!

This Is Why

Dishwashing liquids contain more ingredients called *surfactants,* which produce bubbles. Baby shampoo contains only small amounts of surfactants.

Behold: Bodacious Bubbles!

When your little ones experiment with different kinds of bubble blowers, a bounty of bubbles will result! In advance, put your favorite bubble solution in your water table; then gather a variety of bubble blowers (see the list at right). Have each child predict which bubble blower will make the smallest, largest, and most bubbles. Invite him to use different bubble blowers and then compare the results. Your water table is sure to be a "pop-ular" place!

Bubble blowers to try:
plastic cookie cutters
sunglasses without the lenses
squares of plastic mesh produce bag
plastic funnels
mesh flyswatters
plastic drinking straws
plastic embroidery hoops
large plastic thread spools

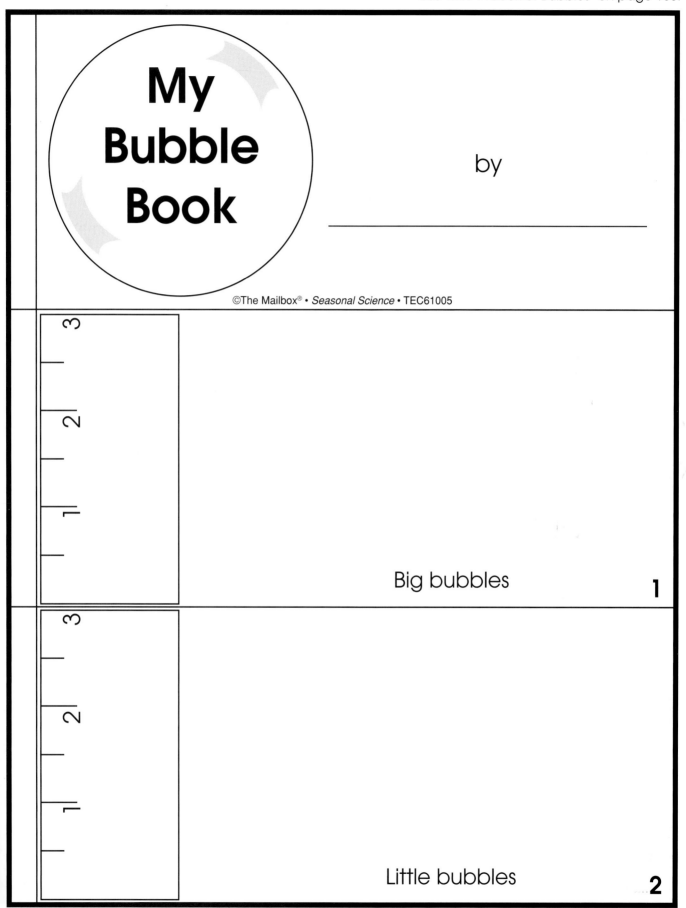

My
Bubble
Book

by

_____

©The Mailbox® • *Seasonal Science* • TEC61005

Big bubbles

1

Little bubbles

2

Butterfly Pattern
Use with "'Bubble-fly' Art" on page 157.

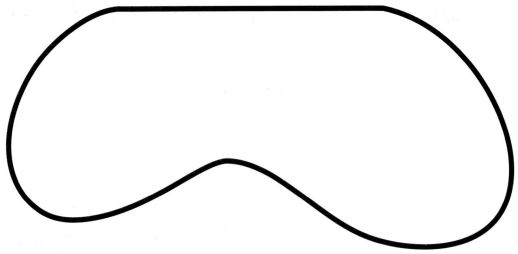

Booklet Pages 3 and 4
Use with "A Book of Bubbles" on page 158.

Bubbles...one, two, three.

3

Here are bubbles blown by me!

4